Letters From a Farmer in Pennsylvania, to the Inhabitants of the British Colonies. The Third Edition

LETTERS

FROM A

FARMER

IN

PENNSYLVANIA,

TO THE

INHABITANTS

OF THE

BRITISH COLONIES.

THE THIRD EDITION.

PHILADELPHIA:

Printed by WILLIAM and THOMAS BRADFORD, at the London *Coffee-House.*   M,DCC,LXIX.

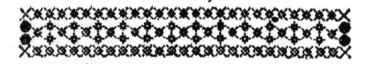

LETTERS

FROM A

FARMER, &c.

LETTER I.

My dear COUNTRYMEN,

I AM a *Farmer*, fettled, after a variety of fortunes, near the banks of the river *Delaware*, in the province of *Pennfylvania*. I received a liberal education, and have been engaged in the bufy fcenes of life ; but am now convinced, that a man may be as happy without buftle, as with it. My farm is fmall ; my fervants are few, and good ; I have a little money at intereft , I wifh for no more ; my employment in my own affairs is eafy ; and with a contented grateful mind, undifturbed by wordly hopes or fears, relating to myfelf, I am completing the number of days allotted to me by divine goodnefs.

BEING generally mafter of my time, I fpend a good deal of it in a library, which I think the moft valuable part of my fmall eftate , and being acquainted with two or three gentlemen of abilities and learning, who honour me with their friendfhip, I have acquired, I believe, a greater knowledge in hiftory, and the laws and conftitution of my country, than is generally attained by men of my clafs, many of them not being fo fortunate as I have been in the opportunities of getting information.

A   FROM

FROM my infancy I was taught to love *humanity* and *liberty*. Enquiry and experience have fince confirmed my reverence for the leffons then given me, by convincing me more fully of their truth and excellence. Benevolence towards mankind, excites wifhes for their welfare, and fuch wifhes endear the means of fulfilling them. *Thefe* can be found in liberty only, and therefore her facred caufe ought to be efpoufed by every man, on every occafion, to the utmoft of his power. As a charitable, but poor perfon does not withhold his *mite*, becaufe he cannot relieve *all* the diftreffes of the miferable, fo fhould not any honeft man fupprefs his fentiments concerning freedom, however fmall their influence is likely to be. Perhaps he " may " touch fome wheel, * " that will have an effect greater than he could reafonably expect.

THESE being my fentiments, I am encouraged to offer to you, my countrymen, my thoughts on fome late tranfactions, that appear to me to be of the utmoft importance to you. Confcious of my own defects, I have waited fome time, in expectation of feeing the fubject treated by perfons much better qualified for the tafk; but being therein difappointed, and apprehenfive that longer delays will be injurious, I venture at length to requeft the attention of the public, praying, that thefe lines may be *read* with the fame zeal for the happinefs of *Britifh America*, with which they were *wrote*.

WITH a good deal of furprize I have obferved, that little notice has been taken of an act of parliament, as injurious in its principle to the liberties of thefe colonies, as the *Stamp-Act* was · I mean the act for fufpending the legiflation of *New-York*.

THE

* POPE

THE affembly of that government complied with a former act of parliament, requiring certain provifions to be made for the troops in *America*, in every particular, I think, except the articles of falt, pepper and vinegar. In my opinion they acted imprudently, confidering all circumftances, in not complying fo far as would have given fatisfaction, as feveral colonies did : But my diflike of their conduct in that inftance, has not blinded me fo much, that I cannot plainly perceive, that they have been punifhed in a manner pernicious to *American* freedom, and juftly alarming to all the colonies.

IF the *Britifh* parliament has a legal authority to iffue an order, that we fhall furnifh a fingle article for the troops here, and to compel obedience to *that* order, they have the fame right to iffue an order for us to fupply thofe troops with arms, cloths, and every neceffary ; and to compel obedience to *that* order alfo; in fhort, to lay *any burthens* they pleafe upon us. What is this but *taxing* us at a *certain fum*, and leaving to us only the *manner* of raifing it ? How is this mode more tolerable than the *Stamp-Act* ? Would that act have appeared more pleafing to *Americans*, if being ordered thereby to raife the fum total of the taxes, the mighty privilege had been left to them, of faying how much fhould be paid for an inftrument of writing on paper, and how much for another on parchment ?

AN act of parliament, commanding us to do a certain thing, if it has any validity, is a *tax* upon us for the expence that accrues in complying with it ; and for this reafon, I believe, every colony on the continent, that chofe to give a mark of their refpect for *Great-Britain*, in complying with the act relating to the troops, cautioufly avoided the mention of that act, left their conduct fhould be attributed to its fuppofed obligation.

THE

THE matter being thus stated, the assembly of *New-York* either had, or had not, a right to refuse submission to that act. If they had, and I imagine no *American* will say they had not, then the parliament had *no right* to compel them to execute it. If they had not *this right*, they had *no right* to punish them for not executing it ; and therefore *no right* to suspend their legislation, which is a punishment. In fact, if the people of *New-York* cannot be legally taxed but by their own representatives, they cannot be legally deprived of the privilege of legislation, only for insisting on that exclusive privilege of taxation. If they may be legally deprived in such a case, of the privilege of legislation, why may they not, with equal reason, be deprived of every other privilege ? Or why may not every colony be treated in the same manner, when any of them shall dare to deny their assent to any impositions, that shall be directed ? Or what signifies the repeal of the *Stamp-Act*, if these colonies are to lose their *other* privileges, by not tamely surrendering *that* of taxation ?

THERE is one consideration arising from this suspension, which is not generally attended to, but shews its importance very clearly. It was not *necessary* that this suspension should be caused by an act of parliament. The crown might have restrained the governor of *New-York*, even from calling the assembly together, by its prerogative in the royal governments. This step, I suppose, would have been taken, if the conduct of the assembly of *New-York* had been regarded as an act of disobedience *to the crown alone* ; but it is regarded as an act of † " disobedience to the authority " of the BRITISH LEGISLATURE " This gives the suspension a consequence vastly more affecting. It is a parliamentary assertion of the *supreme authority* of the *British* legislature over these colonies, in *the point of taxation,*

---

† See the act of suspension.

taxation, and is intended to COMPEL *New-York* into a submission to that authority. It seems therefore to me as much a violation of the liberties of the people of that province, and consequently of all these colonies, as if the parliament had sent a number of regiments to be quartered upon them till they should comply. For it is evident, that the suspension is meant as a *compulsion* ; and the *method* of compelling is totally indifferent. It is indeed probable, that the sight of red coats, and the hearing of drums, would have been most alarming ; because people are generally more influenced by their eyes and ears, than by their reason. But whoever seriously considers the matter, must perceive that a dreadful stroke is aimed at the liberty of these colonies. I say, of these colonies ; for the cause of *one* is the cause of *all*. If the parliament may lawfully deprive *New York* of any of *her* rights, it may deprive any, or all the other colonies of *their* rights ; and nothing can possible so much encourage such attempts, as a mutual inattention to the interests of each other. *To divide, and thus to destroy*, is the first political maxim in attaching those, who are powerful by their union. He certainly is not a wise man, who folds his arms, and reposes himself at home, viewing, with unconcern, the flames that have invaded his neighbour's house, without using any endeavours to extinguish them. When Mr. *Hampden*'s ship money cause, for *Three Shillings* and *Four-pence*, was tried, all the people of *England*, with anxious expectations, interested themselves in the important decision; and when the slightest point, touching the freedom of *one* colony, is agitated, I earnestly wish, that *all the rest* may, with equal ardour, support their sister   Very much may be said on this subject , but I hope, more at present is unnecessary.

WITH concern I have observed, that *two* assemblies of this province have sat and adjourned, without taking any notice of this act. It may perhaps be asked, what
would

would have been proper for them to do? I am by no means fond of inflammatory measures; I detest them. I should be sorry that any thing should be done, which might justly displease our sovereign, or our mother country: But a firm, modest exertion of a free spirit, should never be wanting on public occasions. It appears to me, that it would have been sufficient for the assembly, to have ordered our agents to represent to the King's ministers, their sense of the suspending act, and to pray for its repeal. Thus we should have borne our testimony against it; and might therefore reasonably expect that, on a like occasion, we might receive the same assistance from the other colonies.

Concordia res parvæ crescunt.
Small things grow great by concord.

A FARMER.

* *Nov.* 5.

† The day of King WILLIAM the Third's landing.

LETTER II.

My dear COUNTRYMEN,

THERE is another late act of parliament, which appears to me to be unconstitutional, and as destructive to the liberty of these colonies, as that mentioned in my last letter; that is, the act for granting the duties on paper, glass, &c.

THE parliament unquestionably possesses a legal authority to *regulate* the trade of *Great-Britain*, and all her colonies. Such an authority is essential to the relation between a mother country and her colonies; and necessary for the common good of all. He, who considers these provinces as states distinct from the *British Empire*, has very slender notions of *justice*, or of their *interests*. We are but parts of a *whole*; and therefore there must exist a power somewhere to preside, and preserve the connection in due order. This power is lodged in the parliament; and we are as much dependent on *Great-Britain*, as a perfectly free people can be on another.

I HAVE looked over *every statute* relating to these colonies, from their first settlement to this time; and I find every one of them founded on this principle, till the *Stamp-Act* administration *. *All before*, are calculated
lated

---

* For the satisfaction of the reader, recitals from the former acts of parliament relating to these colonies are added. By comparing these with the modern acts, he will perceive their great difference in *expression* and *intention*.

The 12th *Cha.* Chap. 18, which forms the foundation of the laws relating to *our* trade, by enacting that certain productions of the colonies should be carried to *England* only, and that no goods shall be imported from the plantations but in ships belonging to *England, Ireland, Wales, Berwick*, or the *Plantations, &c.* begins thus ' *For the increase of shipping, and encouragement of the navigation of this nation*, wherein, under the good providence and protection of *GOD*, the wealth, *safety*, and strength of this kingdom is so much concerned," &c.   The

lated to regulate trade, and preferve or promote a mutually beneficial intercourfe between the feveral conftituent parts of the empire ; and though many of them impofed duties on trade, yet thofe duties were always impofed *with defign* to reftrain the commerce of one part, that was injurious to another, and thus to promote

the

The 15th *Cha* II. Chap 7, enforcing the fame regulation, affigns thefe reafons for it. " In regard his Majefty's plantations, beyond the feas, are inhabited and peopled by his fubjects of this his kingdom of *England* ; *for the maintaining a greater correfpondence and kindnefs between them*, and keeping them in a firmer dependence upon it, and rendering them yet more beneficial and advantageous unto it, *in the further employment and increafe of* Englifh *fhipping and feamen*, vent of *Englifh* woollen, and other manufactures and commodities, *rendering the navigation to and from the fame more fafe and cheap*, and making this kingdom a *ftaple*, not only of the commodities of thofe plantations, but alfo of the commodities of other countries and places *for the fupplying of them* , and it being the *ufage* of other nations to keep their plantations trade to themfelves," &c

The 25th *Cha*. II. Chap. 7. made exprefly " *for the better fecuring the plantation trade*," which impofes duties on certain commodities exported from one colony to another, men ions this caufe for impofing them : " Whereas by one act, paffed in the 12th year of your Majefty's reign, intituled, An act for *encouragement of fhipping and navigation*, and by feveral other laws, paffed fince that time, it is permitted to fhip, &c fugars, tobacco, &c of the growth, &c of any of your Majefty's plantations in *America*, &c. from the places of their growth, &c. to any other of your Majefty's plantations in thofe parts, &c. and that *without paying cuftom for the fame*, either at the lading or unlading the faid commodities, by means whereof the trade and navigation in thofe commodities, from one plantation to another, is greatly increafed, and the inhabitants of divers of thofe colonies, *not contenting themfelves with being fupplied with thofe commodities for their own ufe, free from all cuftoms* (while the fubjects of this your kingdom of *England* have paid great cuftoms and impofitions for what of them hath been fpent here) *but, contrary to the exprefs letter of the aforefaid laws, have brought into divers parts of* Europe great quantities thereof, and do alfo vend great quantities thereof to the fhipping of other nations, who bring them into divers parts of *Europe*, to the great hurt and diminution of your Majefty's cuftoms, and of the *trade and navigation* of this your kingdom, FOR THE PREVENTION THEREOF, &c.

The 7th and 8th *Will* III Chap 22, intituled, " An act for preventing frauds, and regulating abufes in the plantation trade," recites that, " notwithftanding divers acts, &c great abufes are daily committed *to the prejudice of the* Englifh *navigation, and the lofs of a great part of the plantation trade* to this kingdom, by the *artifice* and *cunning* of ill difpofed perfons; FOR REMEDY WHEREOF, &c. And whereas in fome of his Majefty's *American* plantations, a doubt or mifconftruction has arifen upon the before mentioned act, made in the 25th year of the reign of

King

the general welfare. The raising a revenue thereby
was never intended. Thus the King, by his judges
in his courts of justice, imposes, fines which all together amount to a very considerable sum, and contribute to the support of government : But this is merely
a consequence arising from restrictions, that only meant
to keep peace, and prevent confusion ; and surely a
man would argue very loosely, who should conclude
from hence, that the King has a right to levy money
in

B

King *Charles* II. whereby certain duties are laid upon the commodities
therein enumerated (which by law may be transported from one plantation to another, for the supply of each others wants) *as if* the same
were, by the payment of those duties in one plantation, discharged from
giving the securities intended by the aforesaid acts, made in the 12th,
22d and 23d years of the reign of King *Charles* the II and consequently
be at liberty to go to any foreign market in *Europe*," &c.

The 6th *Anne*, Chap. 37, reciting the advancement of trade, and
encouragement of ships of war, &c grants to the captors the property
of all prizes carried into *America*, subject to such customs and duties, as
it the same had been first imported into any part of *Great-Britain*, and
from thence exported, &c.

This was *a gift to persons acting under commissions from the crown*, and
therefore it was reasonable that the *terms* prescribed in that gift, should
be complied with---more especially as the payment of such duties was
intended to give a preference to the productions of *British* colonies, over
those of other colonies. However being found inconvenient to the colonies, about four years afterwards, this act was, *for that reason*, so far
repealed, that by another act " all prize goods, imported into any part
of *Great-Britain*, from any of the plantations, were made liable to such
duties only in *Great-Britain*, as in case they had been of the growth and
produce of the plantations."

The 6th *Geo.* II. Chap. 13, which imposes duties on foreign rum,
sugar and melasses, imported into the colonies, shews the reasons thus---
" Whereas the welfare and prosperity of your Majesty's sugar colonies
in *America*, are of the greatest consequence and importance to the *trade,
navigation* and *strength* of this kingdom ; and whereas the planters of the
said sugar colonies, have of late years *fallen into such great discouragements,*
that they are unable to improve or carry on the sugar trade, *upon an
equal footing* with the foreign sugar colonies, *without some advantage and
relief be given to them from* Great-Britain FOR REMEDY WHEREOF,
AND FOR THE GOOD AND WELFARE OF YOUR MAJESTY'S SUBJECTS,"
&c

The 29th *Geo* II Chap 26, and the 1st *Geo*. III Chap. 9, which
continue the 6th *Geo* II. Chap. 13, declare, that the said act hath, by
experience, been found *useful* and *beneficial*, &c These are all the most
considerable statutes relating to the commerce of the colonies , and it is
thought to be utterly unnecessary to add any observations to these extracts,
to prove that they were all intended *solely as regulations of trade.*

in general upon his subjects. Never did the *British* parliament, till the period above mentioned, think of imposing duties in *America*, FOR THE PURPOSE OF RAISING A REVENUE. Mr. *Grenville* first introduced this language, in the preamble to the 4th of *Geo* III. Chap. 15, which has these words " And whereas it is just and necessary that A REVENUE BE RAISED IN YOUR MAJESTY's SAID DOMINIONS IN AMERICA, *for defraying the expences of defending, protecting, and securing the same*: We your Majesty's most dutiful and loyal subjects, THE COMMONS OF GREAT-BRITAIN, in parliament assembled, being desirous to make some provision in this present session of parliament, TOWARDS RAISING THE SAID REVENUE IN AMERICA, have resolved to GIVE and GRANT unto your Majesty the several rates and duties herein after mentioned," *&c.*

A FEW months after came the *Stamp-Act*, which reciting this, proceeds in the same strange mode of expression, thus—" And whereas it is just and necessary, that provision be made FOR RAISING A FURTHER REVENUE WITHIN YOUR MAJESTY's DOMINIONS IN AMERICA, *towards defraying the said expences*, we your Majesty's most dutiful and loyal subjects, the COMMONS OF GREAT-BRITAIN, *&c.* GIVE and GRANT, *&c.* as before.

THE last act, granting duties upon paper, *&c.* carefully pursues these modern precedents. The preamble is, " Whereas it is expedient THAT A REVENUE SHOULD BE RAISED IN YOUR MAJESTY's DOMINIONS IN AMERICA, *for making a more certain and adequate provision for defraying the charge of the administration of justice, and the support of civil government in such provinces, where it shall be found necessary; and towards the further defraying the expences of defending, protecting and securing the said dominions*, we your Majesty's most dutiful and loyal subjects, the COMMONS OF GREAT-BRITAIN, *&c.* GIVE and GRANT," *&c.* as before.

HERE

HERE we may obferve an authority exprefly claimed
and exerted to impofe duties on thefe colonies ; not for
the regulation of trade ; not for the prefervation or
promotion of a mutually beneficial intercourfe between
the feveral conftituent parts of the empire, heretofore
the *fole objects* of parliamentary inftitutions ; *but for the
fingle purpofe of levying money upon us*

THIS I call an * innovation ; and a moft dangerous
innovation. It may perhaps be objected, that *Great-
Britain* has a right to lay what duties fhe pleafes upon
her † exports, and it makes no difference to us, whether they are paid here or there.

To this I anfwer. Thefe colonies require many
things for their ufe, which the laws of *Great-Britain*
prohibit them from getting any where but from her.
Such are paper and glafs.

THAT we may legally be bound to pay any *general*
duties on thefe commodities relative to the regulation of
trade, is granted ; but we being *obliged by the laws* to
take from *Great-Britain,* any *fpecial* duties impofed on
their exportation *to us only, with intention to raife a revenue from us only*, are as much *taxes* upon us, as thofe
impofed by the *Stamp-Act.*

B 2 WHAT

---

* " It is worthy obfervation how quietly fubfidies, granted in forms
ufual and *accuftomable* (though heavy) are borne ; fuch a power hath
ufe and cuftom. On the other fide, what difcontentments and diftur-
bances fubfidies *framed in a new mould* do raife (SUCH AN INBRED HAT-
RED NOVELTY DOTH HATCH) is evident by examples of former times."
Lord *Cooke*'s 2d Inftitute, p 33.

† Some people think that *Great-Britain* has the fame right to impofe
duties on the exports to thefe colonies, as on the exports to *Spain* and
Portugal, &c. Such perfons attend fo much to the idea of exportation,
that they entirely drop *that of the connection between the mother country
and her colonies.* If *Great-Britain* had always claimed, and exercifed
an authority to compel *Spain* and *Portugal* to import manufactures
from her only, the cafes would be parallel : But as fhe never pretended
to fuch a right, they are at liberty to get them where they pleafe, and if
they chufe to take them from her, rather than from other nations, they
voluntarily confent to pay the duties impofed on them.

WHAT is the difference in *substance* and *right*, whether the same sum is raised upon us by the rates mentioned in the *Stamp-Act*, on the *use* of paper, or by these duties, on the *importaton* of it. It is only the edition of a former book, shifting a sentence from the *end* to the *beginning*.

SUPPOSE the duties were made payable in *Great-Britain*

IT signifies nothing to us, whether they are to be paid here or there. Had the *Stamp-Act* directed, that all the paper should be landed at *Florida*, and the duties paid there, before it was brought to the *British* colonies, would the act have raised less money upon us, or have been less destructive of our rights ? By no means : For as we were under a necessity of using the paper, we should have been under the necessity of paying the duties. Thus, in the present case, a like *necessity* will subject us, if this act continues in force, to the payment of the duties now imposed.

WHY was the *Stamp-Act* then so pernicious to freedom ? It did not enact, that every man in the colonies *should* buy a certain quantity of paper——No : It only directed, that no instrument of writing should be valid in law, if not made on stamped paper, &c.

THE makers of that act knew full well, that the confusions that would arise from the disuse of writings, would COMPEL the colonies to use the stamped paper, and therefore to pay the taxes imposed. For this reason the *Stamp-Act* was said to be a law THAT WOULD EXE-CUTE ITSELF. For the very same reason, the last act of parliament, if it is granted to have any force here, WILL EXECUTE ITSELF, and will be attended with the very same consequences to *American* liberty.

SOME

SOME perfons perhaps may fay, that this act lays us under no neceffity to pay the duties impofed, becaufe we may ourfelves manufacture the articles on which they are laid; whereas by the *Stamp-Act* no inftrument of writing could be good, unlefs made on *Britifh* paper, and that too ftamped.

SUCH an objection amounts to no more than this, that the injury refulting to thefe colonies, from the total difufe of *Britifh* paper and glafs, will not be *fo afflicting* as that which would have refulted from the total difufe of writing among them ; for by that means even the *Stamp-Act* might have been eluded. Why then was it univerfally detefted by them as flavery itfelf? Becaufe it prefented to thefe devoted provinces nothing but a * choice of calamities, imbittered by indignities, each of which it was unworthy of freemen to bear. But is no injury a violation of right but the *greateft* injury ? If the eluding the payment of the taxes impofed by the *Stamp-Act*, would have fubjected us to a more dreadful inconvenience, than the eluding the payment of thofe impofed by the late act ; does it therefore follow, that the laft is *no violation* of our rights, tho' it is calculated for the fame purpofe the other was, that is, *to raife money upon us*, WITHOUT OUR CONSENT.

THIS would be making *right* to confift, not in an exemption from *injury*, but from a certain *degree of injury*.

BUT the objectors may further fay, that we fhall fuffer no injury at all by the difufe of *Britifh* paper and glafs. We might not, if we could make as much as we want. But can any man, acquainted with *America*, believe this poffible ? I am told there are but two or three *Glafs-Houfes* on this continent, and but very few
Paper-

* Either the *difufe* of writing, or the payment of *taxes* impofed by pthers *without* our confent.

Paper-Mills ; and suppose more should be erected, a long course of years must elapse, before they can be brought to perfection. This continent is a country of planters, farmers, and fishermen ; not of manufacturers. The difficulty of establishing particular manufactures in such a country, is almost insuperable. For one manufacture is connected with others in such a manner, that it may be said to be impossible to establish one or two, without establishing several others. The experience of many nations may convince us of this truth.

INEXPRESSIBLE therefore must be our distresses in evading the late acts, by the disuse of *British* paper and glass. Nor will this be the extent of our misfortune, if we admit the legality of that act.

GREAT-BRITAIN has prohibited the manufacturing *iron* and *steel* in these colonies, without any objection being made to her *right* of doing it. The *like* right she must have to prohibit any other manufacture among us. Thus she is possessed of an undisputed *precedent* on that point. This authority, she will say, is founded on the *original intention* of settling these colonies ; that is, that we should manufacture for them, and that they should supply her with materials. The *equity* of this policy, she will also say, has been universally acknowledged by the colonies, who never have made the least objections to statutes for that purpose ; and will further appear by the *mutual benefits* flowing from this usage ever since the settlement of these colonies.

OUR great advocate, Mr. *Pitt*, in his speeches on the debate concerning the repeal of the *Stamp-Act*, acknowledged, that *Great-Britain* could restrain our manufactures. His words are these—" This kingdom, as the supreme governing and legislative power, has ALWAYS bound the colonies' by her regulations and RESTRICTIONS in trade, in navigation, in MANUFAC-
TURES

TURES----in every thing, *except that of taking their mo-*
ney out of their pockets, WITHOUT THEIR CONSENT."
Again he fays, " We may bind their trade, CONFINE
THEIR MANUFACTURES, and exercife every power
whatever, *except that of taking their money out of their*
pockets, WITHOUT THEIR CONSENT.

HERE then, my dear countrymen, ROUSE yourfelves, and behold the ruin hanging over your
heads. If you ONCE admit, that *Great-Britain* may
lay duties upon her exportations to us, *for the purpofe*
of levying money on us only, fhe then will have nothing
to do, but to lay thofe duties on the articles which fhe
prohibits us to manutacture---and the tragedy of *Ame-*
rican liberty is finifhed. We have been prohibited
from procuring manufactures, in all cafes, any where
but from *Great-Britain* (excepting linens, which we
are permitted to import directly from *Ireland.*) We
have been prohibited, in fome cafes, from manufacturing for ourfelves ; and may be prohibited in others.
We are therefore exactly in the fituation of a city be-
fieged, which is furrounded by the works of the be-
fiegers in every part *but one.* If *that* is clofed up, no
ftep can be taken, *but to furrender at difcretion.* If
Great-Britain can order us to come to her for necefla-
ries we want, and can order us to pay what taxes fhe
pleafes before we take them away, or when we land
them here, we are as abject flaves as *France* and *Poland*
can fhew in wooden fhoes, and with uncombed hair*.

PERHAPS the nature of the *neceffities* of dependent
ftates, caufed by the policy of a governing one, for her
own benefit, may be elucidated by a fact mentioned in
hiftory. When the *Carthaginians* were poffeffed of the
ifland of *Sardinia,* they made a decree, that the *Sardi-*
nians

---

* The peafants of *France* wear wooden fhoes, and the vaffals of
Poland are remarkable for matted hair, which never can be combed.

nians should not raise *corn*, nor get it any other way than from the *Carthaginians*. Then, by imposing any duties they would upon it, they drained from the miserable *Sardinians* any sums they pleased ; and whenever that oppressed people made the least movement to assert their liberty, their tyrants starved them to death or submission. This may be called the most perfect kind of political necessity.

FROM what has been said, I think this uncontrovertible conclusion may be deduced, that when a ruling state obliges a dependent state to take certain commodities from her alone, it is implied in the nature of that obligation ; is essentially requisite to give it the least degree of justice ; and is inseparably united with it, in order to preserve any share of freedom to the dependent state; *that those commodities should never be loaded with duties*, FOR THE SOLE PURPOSE OF LEVYING MONEY ON THE DEPENDENT STATE.

UPON the whole, the single question is, whether the parliament can legally impose duties to be paid *by the people of these colonies only*, FOR THE SOLE PURPOSE OF RAISING A REVENUE, *on commoditie which she obliges us to take from her alone*, or, in other words, whether the parliament can legally take money out of our pockets, without our consent. If they can, our boasted liberty is but

Vox et præterea nihil.
A sound and nothing else.

A FARMER.

LET-

LETTER III.

My dear COUNTRYMEN,

I REJOICE to find that my two former letters to you, have been generally received with so much favour by such of you, whose sentiments I have had an opportunity of knowing. Could you look into my heart, you would instantly perceive a zealous attachment to your interests, and a lively resentment of every insult and injury offered to you, to be the motives that have engaged me to address you.

I AM no further concerned in any thing affecting *America*, than any one of you, and when liberty leaves it, I can quit it much more conveniently than most of you: But while Divine Providence, that gave me existence in a land of freedom, permits my head to think, my lips to speak, and my hand to move, I shall so highly and gratefully value the blessing received, as to take care, that my silence and inactivity shall not give my implied assent to any act, degrading my brethren and myself from the birthright, wherewith heaven itself " *hath made us free**."

SORRY I am to learn, that there are some few persons, who shake their heads with solemn motion, and pretend to wonder, what can be the meaning of these letters. " *Great-Britain*," They say, " is too powerful to contend with; she is determined to oppress us; it is in vain to speak of right on one side, when there's power on the other; when we are strong enough to resist, we shall attempt it, but now we are not strong enough, and therefore we had better be quiet, it signifies nothing to convince us that our rights are invaded, when we cannot defend them; and if we should

C

get

* GAL. V I.

get into riots and tumults about the late act, it will only draw down heavier displeasure upon us."

WHAT can such men design? What do their grave observations amount to, but this-- " that these colonies, totally regardless of their liberties, should commit them, with humble resignation, to *chance*, *time*, and the tender mercies of *ministers*."

ARE these men ignorant, that usurpations, which might have been successfully opposed at first, acquire strength by continuance, and thus become irresistible? Do they condemn the conduct of these colonies, concerning the *Stamp-Act*? Or have they forgot its successful issue? Ought the colonies at that time, instead of acting as they did, to have trusted for relief to the fortuitous events of futurity? If it is needless " to speak of rights" now, it was as needless then. If the behavior of the colonies was prudent and glorious then, and successful too; it will be equally prudent and glorious to act in the same manner now, if our rights are equally invaded, and may be as successful. Therefore it becomes necessary to enquire, whether " our rights *are* invaded." To talk of ' defending" them, as if they could be no otherwise " defended" than by arms, is as much out of the way, as if a man having a choice of several roads to reach his journey's end, should prefer the worst, for no other reason, but because it *is* the worst.

As to " riots and tumults," the gentlemen who are so apprehensive of them, are much mistaken, if they think, that grievances cannot be redressed without such assistance.

I WILL now tell the gentlemen, what is, " the meaning of these letters." The meaning of them is, to convince the people of these colonies, that they are at this
moment

moment expofed to the moft imminent dangers; and to perfuade them immediately, vigoroufly, and unanimoufly, to exert themfelves, in the moft firm, but moft peaceable manner, for obtaining relief.

THE caufe of *liberty* is a caufe of too much dignity to be fullied by turbulence and tumult. It ought to be maintained in a manner fuitable to her nature Thofe who engage in it, fhould breathe a fedate, yet fervent fpirit, animating them to actions of prudence, juftice, modefly, bravery, humanity and magnanimity.

To fuch a wonderful degree were the antient *Spartans*, as brave and free a people as ever exifted, infpired by this happy temperature of foul, that rejecting even in their battles the ufe of trumpets, and other inftruments for exciting heat and rage they marched up to fcenes of havock, and horror*, with the found of flutes, to the tunes of which their fteps kept pace---" exhibiting," as *Plutarch* fays, " at once a terrible and delightful fight, and proceeding with a deliberate valor, full of hope and good affurance, as if fome divinity had fenfibly affifted them "

I HOPE, my dear countrymen, that you will, in every colony, be upon your guard againft thofe, who may at any time endeavour to ftir you up, under pretences of patriotifm, to any meafures difrefpectful to our Sovereign and our mother country. Hot, rafh, diforderly proceedings, injure the reputation of a people, as to wifdom, valor and virtue, without procuring them the leaft benefit I pray GOD, that he may be pleafed to infpire you and your pofterity, to the lateft ages, with a fpirit of which I have an idea, that I find a difficulty to exprefs. To exprefs it in the beft manner I can, I mean a fpirit, that fhall fo guide you, that

C 2 it

* *Plutarch* in the life of *Lycurgus* Archbifhop Potter's Archæologia Græca.

it will be impoffible to determine whether an *American's* character is moft diftinguifhable, for his loyalty to his Sovereign, his duty to his mother country, his love of freedom, or his affection for his native foil.

EVERY government at fome time or other falls into wrong meafures. Thefe may proceed from miftake or paffion. But every fuch meafure does not diffolve the obligation between the governors and the governed. The miftake may be corrected, the paffion may fubfide. I. is the duty of the governed to endeavour to rectify the miftake, and to appeafe the paffion. They have not at firft any other right, than to reprefent their grievances, and to pray for redrefs, unlefs an emergence is fo preffing, as not to allow time for receiving an anfwer to their applications, which rarely happens. If their applications are difregarded, then that kind of *oppofition* becomes juftifiable, which can be made without breaking the laws, or difturbing the public peace.

THIS confifts in the *prevention of the oppreffors reaping advantage from their oppreffions*, and not in their punifhment For experience may teach them, what reafon did not; and harfh methods cannot be proper, till milder ones have failed.

IF at length it become, UNDOUBTED, that an inveterate refolution is formed to annihilate the liberties of the governed, the *Englifh* hiftory affords frequent examples of refiftance by force What particular circumftances will in any future cafe juftify fuch refiftance, can never be afcertained, till they happen Perhaps it may be allowable to fay generally, that it never can be juftifiable, until the people are FULLY CONVINCED, that any further fubmiffion will be deftructive to their happinefs.

WHEN

WHEN the appeal is made to the fword, highly probable is it, that the punifhment will exceed the offence; and the calamities attending on war out-weigh thofe preceeding it. Thefe confiderations of juftice and prudence, will always have great influence with good and wife men.

To thefe reflections on this fubject, it remains to be added, and ought for ever to be remembered, that refiftance, in the cafe of colonies againft their mother country, is extremely different from the refiftance of a people againft their prince. A nation may change their king, or race of kings, and, retaining their antient form of government, be gainers by changing. Thus *Great-Britain*, under the illuftrious houfe of *Brunfwick*, a houfe that feems to flourifh for the happinefs of mankind, has found a felicity, unknown in the reigns of the *Stewarts*. But if once *we* are feparated from our mother country, what new form of government fhall we adopt, or where fhall we find another *Britain*, to fupply our lofs? Torn from the body, to which we are united by religion, liberty, laws, affections, relation, language and commerce, we muft bleed at every vein.

IN truth---the profperity of thefe provinces is founded in their dependence on *Great-Britain*, and when fhe returns to her " old good humour, and her old good nature," as Lord *Clarendon* expreffes it, I hope they will always think it their duty and intereft, as it moft certainly will be, to promote her welfare by all the means in their power.

WE cannot act with too much caution in our difputes. Anger produces anger, and differences, that might be accommodated by kind and refpectful behahavior, may, by imprudence, be enlarged to an incurable rage. In quarrels between countries, as well as

in

in thofe between individuals, when they have rifen to a certain heighth, the firft caufe of diffenfion is no longer remembered, the minds of the parties being wholly engaged in recollecting and refenting the mutual expreffions of their diflike. When feuds have reached that fatal point, all confiderations of reafon and equity vanifh; and a blind fury governs, or rather confounds all things. A people no longer regards their intereft, but the gratification of their wrath. The fway of the ‡ *Cleons* and *Clodius*'s, the defigning and deftable flatterers of the *prevailing paffion*, becomes confirmed. Wife and good men in vain oppofe the ftorm, and may think themfelves fortunate, if, in attempting to preferve their ungrateful fellow citizens, they do not ruin themfelves. Their *prudence* will be called *bafenefs*; their *moderation* will be called *guilt*; and if their virtue does not lead them to deftruction, as that of many other great and excellent perfons has done, they may furvive to receive from their expiring country the mournful glory of her acknowledgment, that their counfels, if regarged, would have faved her.

The conftitutional modes of obtaining relief, are thofe which I wifh to fee purfued on the prefent occafion; that is, by petitions of our affemblies, or where they are not permitted to meet, of the people, to the powers that can afford us relief.

We have an excellent prince, in whofe good difpofitions towards us we may confide. We have a generous, fenfible and humane nation, to whom we may apply. They may be deceived. They may, by artful men, be provoked to anger againft us. I cannot believe they will be cruel or unjuft; or that their anger will be implacable. Let us behave like dutiful children, who have received unmerited blows from a be-
loved

---

‡ *Cleon* was a popular firebrand of *Athens*, and *Clodus* of *Rome*, each of whom plunged his country into the deepeft calamities

loved parent. Let us complain to our parent; but let our complaints speak at the same time the language of affliction and veneration.

If, however, it shall happen, by an unfortunate course of affairs, that our applications to his Majesty and the parliament for redress, prove ineffectual, let us THEN take *another step*, by withholding from *Great-Britain* all the advantages she has been used to receive from us. THEN let us try, if our ingenuity, industry, and frugality, will not give weight to our remonstrances. Let us all be united with one spirit, in one cause. Let us invent---let us work---let us save---let us, continually, keep up our claim, and incessantly repeat our complaints---But, above all, let us implore the protection of that infinitely good and gracious being, † "by whom kings reign, and princes decree justice."

Nil desperandum.

Nothing is to be despaired of.

A FARMER.

† Pro. viii. 15.

LET-

LETTER IV.

My dear COUNTRYMEN,

AN objection, I hear, has been made against my second letter, which I would willingly clear up before I proceed. " There is," say these objectors, " a material difference between the *Stamp-Act* and the *late Act* for laying a duty on paper, *&c.* that justifies the conduct of those who opposed the former, and yet are willing to submit to the latter. The duties imposed by the *Stamp-Act* were *internal* taxes; but the present are *external,* and therefore the parliament may have a right to impose them."

To this I answer, with a total denial of the power of parliament to lay upon these colonies any " *tax*" whatever.

THIS point, being so important to this, and to succeeding generations, I wish to be clearly understood.

To the word " *tax*," I annex that meaning which the constitution and history of *England* require to be annexed to it, that is —that it is *an imposition on the subject, for the sole purpose of levying money.*

IN the early ages of our monarchy, certain services were rendered to the crown *for the general good.* These were personal*: But in process of time, such institutions

---

* It is very worthy of remark how watchful our wise ancestors were, lest their *services* should be encreased beyond what the law allowed. No man was bound to go out of the realm to serve the King. Therefore, even in the conquering reign of *Henry* the *Fifth,* when the martial spirit of the nation was nobly enflamed by the heroic courage of their Prince, and by his great success they still carefully guarded against the establishment of illegal services. ' When this point (says Lord Chief Justice *Coke*) concerning maintenance of wars out of *England,* came in question, the COMMONS did make their *continual claim* of their

bns being found inconvenient, *gifts* and *grants* of their bwn property were made by the people, under the several names of aids, tallages, tasks, taxes and subsidies, &c. These were made, as may be collected even from the names, *for public service* upon " need and necessity ‡." All these sums were levied upon the people by virtue of their voluntary gift *. Their design was to support the *national honor and interest* Some of those grants comprehended duties arising from trade; being imposts on merchandizes. These Lord Chief Justice *Coke* classes under " subsidies," and " parliamentary aids." They are also called " customs." But

whatever

D

their *ancient freedom* and *birthright*, as in the first of *Henry the Fifth*, and in the seventh of *Henry the Fifth*, &c. the COMMONS made a PROTEST, that they were not bound to the maintenance of war in *Scotland*, *Ireland*, *Calice*, *France*, *Normandy*, or other *foreign* parts, and caused their PROTESTS to be entered into the parliament rolls, where they yet remain; which, in effect, agreeth with that which, upon like occasion, was made in the parliament of 25th *Edward* I." 2d Inst. p. 528.

‡ 4th Inst. p. 28.
* *Reges* Angliæ, *nihil tale, nisi convocatis primis ordinibus, et assentiente populo suscipiunt.* Phil. Comines, 2d *Inst*

These gifts entirely depending on the pleasure of the donors, were proportioned to the abilities of the several ranks of people who gave, and were regulated by *their* opinion of the public necessities. Thus *Edward* I had in his 11th year a *thirtieth* from the *laity*, a *twentieth* from the *clergy*; in his 22d year, a *tenth* from the *laity*, a *sixth* from *London*, and other corporate towns, *half of their benefices* from the *clergy*, in his 23d year an *eleventh* from the *barons* and others, a *tenth* from the *clergy*, a *seventh* from the *burgesses*, &c Hume's *Hist. of England.*

The same difference in the grants of the several ranks is observable in other reigns.

In the famous statute *de tallagio non concedendo*, the king enumerates the several *classes*, without whose consent, he and his heirs never should set or levy any tax---" *nullum tallagium, vel auxilium per nos, vel heredes nostros in regno nostro ponatur seu levetur, sine voluntate et assensu archiepiscoporum, episcoporum, comitum, baronum, militum, burgensium, et aliorum liberorum com. de regno nostro.*" 34th *Edward* I

Lord Chief Justice *Coke*, in his comment on these words says --for the quieting of the *commons*, and for a *perpetual and constant law for ever after*, both in this AND OTHER LIKE CASES, this act was made. These words are *plain*, WITHOUT ANY SCRUPLE, *absolute*, WITHOUT ANY SAVING." 2d *Coke's* Inst p 532, 533 Little did the venerable judge imagine, that " *other* LIKE *cases*" would happen, in which the spirit of this law would be despised by *Englishmen*, the posterity of those who made it.

whatever the *name* was, they were always confidered as *gifts of the people to the crown, to be employed for public ufes.*

COMMERCE was at a low ebb, and furprizing inftances might be produced how little it was attended to for a fucceffion of ages. The terms that have been mentioned, and, among the reft, that of " *tax,*" had obtained a national, parliamentary meaning, drawn from the principles of the conftitution, long before any *Englifhman* thought of *impofition of duties, for the regulation of trade.*

WHENEVER we fpeak of " taxes" among *Englifhmen,* let us therefore fpeak of them with reference to the *principles* on which, and the *intentions* with which they have been eftablifhed. This will give certainty to our expreffion, and fafety to our conduct: But if, when we have in view the liberty of thefe colonies, we proceed in any other courfe, we purfue a *Juno* * indeed, but fhall only catch a cloud.

IN the national, parliamentary fenfe infifted on, the word " tax §" was certainly underftood by the congrefs at *New-York,* whofe refolves may be faid to form the *American* " bill of rights."

THE third, fourth, fifth, and fixth refolves, are thus expreffed.

III. " THAT it is *infeperably effential to the freedom of a people,* and the *undoubted right* of *Englifhmen,* that † NO
TAX

* The Goddefs of *Empire,* in the Heathen Mythology; according to an antient fable, *Ixion* purfued her, but fhe efcaped in a cloud
§ In this fenfe *Montifquieu* ufes the word " tax," in his 13th book of *Spirit of Laws.*
† The rough draught of the refolves of the congrefs at *New-York* are now in my hands, and from fome notes on that draught, and other particular reafons, I am fatisfied that the congrefs underftood the word " tax" in the fenfe here contended for.

TAX be imposed on them, *but with their own consent,* given personally, or by their representatives."

IV. " THAT the people of the colonies are not, and from their local circumstances, cannot be represented in the house of commons in *Great-Britain.*"

V. " THAT the only representatives of the people of the colonies, are the persons chosen therein by themselves ; and that NO TAXES ever have been, or can be constitutionally imposed on them, but by their respective legislatures."

VI. " THAT ALL *supplies to the crown,* being free gifts of the people, it is *unreasonable, and inconsistent with the principles and spirit of the* British *constitution,* for the people of *Great-Britain to* grant to his Majesty *the property of the colonies.*"

HERE is no distinction made between *internal* and *external* taxes. It is evident from the short reasoning thrown into these resolves, that every imposition " to grant to his Majesty *the property of the colonies,*" was thought a " tax;" and that every such imposition, if laid any other way than " with their consent, given personally, or by their representatives," was not only " unreasonable, and inconsistent with the principles and spirit of the *British* constitution," but destructive " to the freedom of a people."

THIS language is clear and important. A " TAX" means an imposition to raise money. Such persons therefore as speak of *internal* and *external* " TAXES," I pray may pardon me, if I object to that expression, as applied to the privileges and interests of these colonies. There may be *internal* and *external* IMPOSITIONS, founded on *different principles,* and having *different tendencies;*

every

every " tax" being an impofition, tho' every impofition is not a " tax." But *all taxes* are founded on the
fame principle; and have the *fame tendency*.

EXTERNAL impofitions, for the regulation of our
trade, do not " grant to his Majefty *the property of the
colonies*." They only *prevent the colonies acquiring property*, in things not neceffary, in a manner judged to
be injurious to the welfare of the whole empire. But
the laft ftatute refpecting us, " grants to his Majefty
the property of the colonies," by laying duties on the manufactures of *Great-Britain* which they MUST take, and
which fhe fettled on them, on purpofe that they SHOULD
take

WHAT * *tax* can be more *internal* than this ? Here
is money drawn, *without their confent*, from a fociety,
who

* It feems to be evident, that Mr *Pitt*, in his defence of *America*,
during the debate concerning the repeal of the *Stamp Act*, by *internal
taxes*," meant any duties " for the purpofe of raifing a revenue ," and
by " *external* taxes," meant duties impofed " for the regulation of
trade." His expreffions are thefe---" If the gentleman does not underftand the difference between *internal* and *external* taxe', I cannot
help it, but there is a plain diftinction between taxes levied FOR THE
PURPOSES OF RAISING A REVENUE, and duties impofed FOR THE
REGULATION OF TRADE, for the accommodation of the fubject ; al-
though, in the confequences, fome revenue might incidentally arife
from the latter.

Thefe words were in Mr *Pitt's* reply to Mr. *Grenville*, who faid he
could not underftand the difference between external and internal
taxes.

In every other part of his fpeeches on that occafion, his words confirm
this conftruction of his expreffions. The following extracts will fhew
how pofitive and general were his affertions of our right.

" It is my opinion that this kingdom has NO RIGHT to lay A TAX
upon the colonies. '---" The *Americans* are the SONS, not the BAS-
TARDS of *England*. TAXATION IS NO PART of the *governing* and *legif-
lative* power "---" The *taxes* are a voluntary *gift* and *grant* of the *commons* ALONE In LEGISLATION the THREE eftates of the realm are
ALIKE concerned, but the concurrence of the PEERS and the CROWN to
a TAX, is only neceffary to clofe with the FORM of a law. The GIFT
and GRANT is of the COMMONS ALONE "---" *The diftinction between*
LEGISLATION *and* TAXATION *is effentially neceffary to liberty*."---" THE
COMMONS of *America*, reprefented in their feveral affemblies, have ever
been in poffeffion of the exercife of this their conftitutional right, of
GIVING and GRANTING their own MONEY, *They would have been*
SLAVES,

who have conftantly enjoyed a conftitutional mode of
raifing all money among themfelves. The payment
of their *tax* they have no poffible method of avoiding;
as they cannot do without the commodities on which it
is laid, and they cannot manufacture thefe commodities
themfelves. Befides, if this unhappy country fhould
be fo lucky as to elude this act, by getting parchment
enough, in the place of paper, or by reviving the antient method of writing on wax and bark, and by in-
venting fomething to ferve inftead of glafs, her ingenuity would ftand her in little ftead; for then the parliament would have nothing to do but to prohibit fuch
manufactures, or to lay a tax on *hats* and *woollen cloths*,
which they have already prohibited the colonies *from
fupplying each other with*, or on inftruments, and tools
of *fteel* and *iron*, which they have prohibited the pro-
vincials *from manufacturing at all* ‡: And then, what
little

SLAVES, if they had not enjoyed it " " The idea of a *virtual* reprefen-
tation of *America* in this houfe, is the moft contempt.ble idea that ever
entered into the head of man ---It does not deferve a ferious refutation "
He afterwards fhews the unreafonablenefs of *Great-Britain* taxing
America, thus---" When I had the honor of ferving his Majefty, I
availed myfelf of the means of information, which I derived from my
office, I SPEAK THEREFORE FROM KNOWLEDGE My materials were
good I was at pains to *collect*, to *digeft*, to *confider* them; and *I will
be bold to affirm*, that the profit to *Great-Britain* from the trade of the
colonies, through all its branches, is TWO MILLIONS A YEAR. *This is*
the fund that carried you triumphantly through the laft war The
eftates that were rented at two thoufand pounds a year, threefcore
years ago, are three thoufand pounds at prefent Thofe eftates fold
then from fifteen to eighteen years purchafe, the fame may now be
fold for thirty. YOU OWE THIS TO AMERICA THIS IS THE PRICE
THAT AMERICA PAYS YOU FOR HER PROTECTION ---" I dare not
fay how much higher thefe profits may be augmented " --" Upon the
whole, I will beg leave to tell the houfe what is really my opinion, it
is, that the *Stamp Act* be repealed abfolutely, totally, and immediately.
That the reafon for the repeal be affigned, becaufe it was founded on
an ERRONEOUS PRINCIPLE "

‡ " And that *pig* and *bar iron*, made in his Majefty s colonies in
America, may be FURTHER MANUFACTURED IN THIS KINGDOM, be it
further enacted by the authority aforefaid, that from and after the
twenty fourth day of *June*, 1750, no *mill*, or *other engine*, for *flitting*
or *rolling of iron*, or any *plating forge*, to work with a *tilt hammer*, or
any *furnace* for *making fteel*, fhall be erected, or, after fuch erection,
continued IN ANY OF HIS MAJESTY s COLONIES IN AMERICA." 23d
George II. Chap. 29, Sect. 9

little gold and filver they have, muft be torn from
their hands, or they will not be able, in a fhort time,
to get an ax †, for cutting their firewood, nor a plough,
for raifing their food. In what refpect, therefore, I
beg leave to afk, is the late act preferable to the *Stamp-
Act*, or more confiftent with the liberties of the colonies ?. For my own part, I regard them both with equal
apprehenfions; and think they ought to be in the fame
manner oppofed.

> *Habemus quidem fenatus confultum,———tanquam
> gladium in vagina repofitum.*

We have a ftatute, laid up for future ufe, like a
fword in the fcabbard.

A FARMER.

† Tho' thefe particulars are mentioned as being abfolutely neceffary,
yet perhaps they are not more fo than glafs in our fevere winters, to
keep out the cold from our houfes; or than paper, without which fuch
inexpreffible confufions muft enfue.

LET-

L E T T E R V.

My dear COUNTRYMEN,

PERHAPS the objection to the late act, imposing duties upon paper, &c. might have been safely rested on the argument drawn from the universal conduct of parliaments and ministers, from the first existence of these colonies, to the administration of Mr. *Greenville.*

WHAT but the indisputable, the acknowledged exclusive right of the colonies to tax themselves, could be the reason, that in this long period of more than one hundred and fifty years, no statute was ever passed for the sole purpose of raising a revenue on the colonies? And how clear, how cogent must that reason be, to which every parliament, and every minister, for so long a time submitted, without a single attempt to innovate?

ENGLAND, in part of that course of years, and *Great-Britain,* in other parts, was engaged in several fierce expensive wars; troubled with some tumultuous and bold parliaments; governed by many daring and wicked ministers; yet none of them ever ventured to touch the *Palladium* of *American* liberty. Ambition, avarice, faction, tyranny, all revered it. Whenever it was necessary to raise money on the colonies, the requisitions of the crown were made, and dutifully complied with. The parliament, from time to time, regulated their trade, and that of the rest of the empire, to preserve their dependence, and the connection of the whole in good order.

THE people of *Great-Britain,* in support of their privileges, boast much of their antiquity. It is true they are antient; yet it may well be questioned, if there

is

is a single privilege of a *British* subject, supported by longer, more solemn, or more uninterrupted testimony, than the exclusive right of taxation in these colonies. The people of *Great-Britain* consider that kingdom as the sovereign of these colonies, and would now annex to that sovereignty a prerogative never heard of before. How would they bear this, was the case their own? What would they think of a *new* prerogative claimed by the crown? We may guess what their conduct would be, from the transports of passion into which they fell about the late embargo, tho' laid to relieve the most emergent necessities of state, admitting of no delay ; and for which there were numerous precedents. Let our liberties be treated with the same tenderness, and it is all we desire.

EXPLICIT as the conduct of parliaments, for so many ages, is, to prove that no money can be levied on these colonies by parliament, for the purpose of raising a revenue, yet it is not the only evidence in our favour.

EVERY one of the most material arguments against the legality of the *Stamp-Act*, operates with equal force against the act now objected to ; but as they are well known, it seems unnecessary to repeat them here.

THIS general one only shall be considered at present : That tho' these colonies are dependent on *Great-Britain* ; and tho' she has a legal power to make laws for preserving that dependence ; yet it is not necessary for this purpose, nor essential to the relation between a mother country and her colonies, as was eagerly contended by the advocates for the *Stamp-Act*, that she should raise money on them without their consent.

COLONIES were formerly planted by warlike nations, to keep their enemies in awe ; to relieve their country, overburthened with inhabitants; or to discharge a
number

number of difcontented and troublefome citizens. But in more modern ages, the fpirit of violence being in fome meafure, if the expreffion may be allowed, fheathed in commerce, colonies have been fettled by the nations of *Europe* for the purpofes of trade. Thefe purpofes were to be attained, by the colonies raifing for their mother country thofe things which fhe did not produce herfelf; and by fupplying themfelves from her with things they wanted. Thefe were the *national objeEts* in the commencement of our colonies, and have been uniformly fo in their promotion.

To anfwer thefe grand purpofes, perfect liberty was known to be neceffary; all hiftory proving, that trade and freedom are nearly related to each other. By a due regard to this wife and juft plan, the infant colonies, expofed in the unknown climates and unexplored wildernefles of this new world, lived, grew and flourifhed.

THE parent country, with undeviating prudence and virtue, attentive to the firft principles of colonization, drew to herfelf the benefits fhe might reafonably expect, and preferved to her children the bleffings, on which thofe benefits were founded. She made laws, obliging her colonies to carry to her all thofe products which fhe wanted for her own ufe, and all thofe raw materials which fhe chofe herfelf to work up. Befides this reftriction, fhe forbad them to procure *manufaEtures* from any other part of the globe, or even the *produEts* of *European* countries, which alone could rival her, without being firft brought to her. In fhort, by a variety of laws, fhe regulated their trade in fuch a manner as fhe thought moft conducive to their mutual advantage, and her own welfare. A power was referved to the crown of *repealing* any laws that fhould be enacted: The *executive* authority of government was alfo lodged in the crown, and its reprefentatives; and an

E   *appeal*

appeal was fecured to the crown from all judgments in the adminiftration of juftice.

For all thefe powers, eftablifhed by the mother country over the colonies ; for all thefe immenfe emoluments derived by her from them ; for all their difficulties and diftreffes in fixing themfelves, what was the recompence made them ? A communication of her rights in general, and particularly of that great one, the foundation of all the reft---that their property, acquired with fo much pain and hazard, fhould be difpofed of by none but * themfelves---or to ufe the beautiful and emphatic language of the facred fcriptures †, " that they fhould fit *every man* under his vine, and under his fig-tree, and NONE SHOULD MAKE THEM AFRAID."

Can any man of candor and knowledge deny, that thefe inftitutions form an affinity between *Great-Britain* and her colonies, that fufficiently fecures their dependence upon her ? Or that for her to levy taxes upon them, is to reverfe the nature of things ? Or that fhe can purfue fuch a meafure. without reducing them to a ftate of vaffallage ?

If any perfon cannot conceive the fupremacy of *Great-Britain* to exift, without the power of laying taxes to levy money upon us, the hiftory of the colonies, and of *Great-Britain*, fince their fettlement, will prove the contrary. He will there find the amazing advantages arifing to her from them---the conftant exercife of her fupremacy---and their filial fubmiffion to it, without a fingle rebellion, or even the thought of one, from their firft emigration to this moment--- And all thefe things have happened, without one inftance of *Great-Britain*'s laying taxes to levy money upon them.   How

---

* " The power of *taxing themfelves*, was the privilege of which the *Englifh* were, WITH REASON, *particularly jealous*." *Hume's Hift. of England.*   † MIC. IV 4

How many ‡ *British authors* have demonstrated, that the present wealth, power and glory of their country, are founded upon these colonies? As constantly as streams tend to the ocean, have they been pouring the

E 2

‡ It has been said in the House of Commons, when complaints have been made of the decay of trade to any part of *Europe*, " That such things were not worth regard, as *Great-Britain* was possessed of colonies that could consume more of her manufactures than she was able to supply them with."

" As the case now stands, we shall shew that the *plantations* are a spring of *wealth* to this nation, that they *work* for us, that their TREASURE CENTERS ALL HERE, and that the laws have tied them fast enough to us; so that it must be through our own fault and mismanagement, if they become independent of *England* '

DAVENANT *on the Plantation Trade*

" It is better that the islands should be supplied from the Northern Colonies than from *England*, for this reason, the provisions we might send to *Barbados, Jamaica*, &c would be *unimproved* product of the earth, as grain of all kinds, or such product where there is little got by the improvement, as malt, salt beef and pork ; indeed the exportation of salt fish thither would be more advantageous, but the goods which we send to the *Northern Colonies*, are such whose *improvement* may be justly said, one with another, to be near *four fifths* of the value of the *whole commodity*, as apparel, houshold furniture, and many other things " *Idem*

" *New-England* is the most prejudicial plantation to the kingdom of *England*, and yet to do right to that most industrious *English* colony, I must confess, that though we lose by their unlimited trade with other foreign plantations, yet we are very great gainers by their direct trade from *Old England* Our yearly exportation of *English* manufactures, malt and other goods, from hence thither, amounting in my opinion, to *ten times* the value of what is imported from thence, which calculation I do not make at random, but upon *mature confideration*, and, peradventure, upon *as much experience in this very trade*, as any other person will pretend to , and therefore, whenever reformation of our correspondency in trade with that people shall be thought on, it will, in my poor judgment, require GREAT TENDERNESS, and VERY SERIOUS CIRCUMSPECTION " ' *Sir* JOSIAH CHILD's *Discourse on Trade*.

" Our plantations spend mostly our *English* manufactures, and those *of all sorts almost imaginable*, in *egregious quantities*, and employ near *two thirds of all our* English *shipping* ; so that we have *more people* in *England*, by reason of our plantations in *America*. ' *Idem*

Sir JOSIAH CHILD says, in another part of his work, " That not more than fifty families are maintained in *England* by the refining of sugar " From whence, and from what *Davenant* says, it is plain, that the advantages here said to be derived from the plantations by *England* must be meant chiefly of the continental colonies.

I shall turn up my whole remarks on our *American* colonies, with this observation, that as they are a certain annual revenue of SEVERAL MILLIONS

the fruits of all their labors into their mother's lap,
Good heaven! and shall a total oblivion of former ten-
dernesses and blessings, be spread over the minds of a
good and wise nation, by the sordid arts of intriguing
men,

MILLIONS STERLING to their mother country, they ought carefully to
be protected, duly encouraged, and every opportunity that presents, im-
proved for their increment and advantage, as every one they can possi-
bly reap, must at last return to us with interest."
                                    BEAWES's *Lex Merc Red.*

" We may safely advance, that our trade and navigation are greatly
increased by our colonies, and that they really are a source of treasure
and naval power to this kingdom, since THEY WORK FOR US, & THEIR
TREASURE CENTERS HERE   Before their settlement, our manufactures were few, and those but indifferent, the number of *English*
merchants very small, and the whole shipping of the nation much inferior to what now belongs to the Northern Colonies only. *These are
certain facts*   But since their establishment, our condition has altered
for the better, almost of a degree beyond credibility.---Our MANUFAC-
TURES are prodigiously increased, chiefly by the demand for them in
the plantations, where they AT LEAST TAKE OFF ONE HALF, and supply us with many valuable commodities for exportation, which is as
great an emolument to the mother kingdom, as to the plantations themselves."   POSTLETHWAYT *s Univ Dict. of Trade and Commerce.*

" Most of the nations of *Europe* have interfered with us, more or
less, in divers of our staple manufactures, within half a century, not
only in our woollen, but in our lead and tin manufactures, as well as
our fisheries."   POSTLETHWAYT, *ibid.*

" The inhabitants of our colonies, by carrying on a trade with their
foreign neighbours, do not only occasion *a greater quantity of the goods and
merchandize of* Europe *being sent from hence to them*, and a greater quantity of the product of *America* to be sent from them hither, *which
would otherwise be carried from and brought to* Europe *by foreigners*, but
an increase of the seamen and navigation in those parts, which is of
great strength and security, as well as of great advantage to our plantations in general.   And though *some of our colonies* are not only for
preventing the *importation of all goods of the same species they produce*, but
suffer particular planters to *keep great runs of land in their possession uncul-
tivated*, with design to prevent new settlements, whereby they imagine
the prices of their commodities may be affected , yet if it be considered,
that the markets of *Great-Britain* depend on the markets of ALL *Europe
in general*, and that the *European* markets *in general* depend on the proportion between the *annual consumption* and the *whole quantity* of each
species *annually produced* by ALL *nations*; it must follow, that whether
we or foreigners are the producers, *carriers*, importers and exporters
of *American* produce, yet their respective prices in *each colony* (the difference of freight, customs and importations considered) will always
bear proportion to the *general consumption* of the *whole quantity* of each
sort, *produced in all colonies*, and *in all parts*, allowing only for the usual
contingencies that trade and commerce, agriculture and manufactures,
are liable to in all countries,"   POSTLETHWAYT, *ibid.*

                                                            " It

men, who, covering their selfish projects under pretences of public good, first enrage their countrymen into a frenzy of passion, and then advance their own influence and interest, by gratifying the passion, which they themselves have basely excited.

HITHERTO

" It is certain, that from the very time Sir *William Raleigh*, the father of our *English* colonies, and his associates, first projected these establishments, there have been persons who have found an interest, in *misrepresenting*, or lessening the value of them --The attempts were called chimerical and dangerous. Afterwards many malignant suggestions were made about sacrificing so many *Englishmen* to the obstinate desire of settling colonies in countries which then produced very little advantage. But as these difficulties were gradually surmounted, those complaints vanished. No sooner were *those lamentations* over, but *others* arose in their stead ; when it could be no longer said, that the colonies were *useless*, it was alledged that they were not *useful enough* to their mother country , that while we were loaded with taxes, they were absolutely free ; that the *planters* lived like *princes*, while the inhabitants of *England* laboured hard for a tolerable subsistence."

POSTLETHWAYT, *ibid.*

" Before the settlement of these colonies," says *Postlethwayt*, " our manufactures were few, and those but indifferent In those days we had not only our naval stores, but our ships from our neighbours. *Germany* furnished us with all things made of metal, even to nails. Wine, paper, linens, and a thousand other things, came from *France*. *Portugal* supplied us with sugar ; all the products of *America* were poured into us from *Spain* ; and the *Venetians* and *Genoese* retailed to us the commodities of the *East-Indies*, at their own price."

" If it be asked, whether foreigners, for what goods they take of us, do not pay on *that consumption* a great portion of our taxes ? It is admitted they do "   POSTLETHWAYT's *Great Britain's True System.*

" If we are afraid that one day or other the colonies will revolt, and set up for themselves, as some seem to apprehend, let us not *drive* them to a *necessity* to *feel* themselves independent of us , as they *will* do, the moment they perceive that *THEY CAN BE SUPPLIED WITH ALL THINGS FROM WITHIN THEMSELVES*, and do not need our assistance If we would keep them still dependent upon their mother country, and in some respects, *subservient* to her *views* and welfare , let us make it their INTEREST always to be so."

TUCKER *on Trade*

" Our colonies, while they have *English* blood in their veins, and have relations in *England*, and WHILE THEY CAN GET BY TRADING WITH US, the *stronger* and *greater* they grow, the *more* this *crown* and *kingdom* will *get* by them , and nothing but such an arbitrary power as shall make them desperate, can bring them to rebel."

DAVENANT *on the Plantation Trade*

" The Northern colonies are not upon the same footing as those of the South , and having a worse soil to improve, they must find the recompence some other way, which only can be in property and dominion : Upon which score, any INNOVATIONS in the form of government

HITHERTO *Great-Britain* has been contented with her prosperity. Moderation has been the rule of her conduct. But now, a generous humane people, that so often has protected the liberty of *strangers*, is enflamed into an attempt to tear a privilege from her own

ment there, should be cautiously examined, for fear of entering upon measures, by which the industry of the inhabitants be quite discouraged. 'TIS ALWAYS UNFORTUNATE for a people, either by CONSENT, or upon COMPULSION, to depart from their PRIMITIVE INSTITUTIONS, and THOSE FUNDAMENTALS, by which they were FIRST UNITED TOGETHER." *Idem.*

The most effectual way of *uniting* the colonies, is to make it their common interest to oppose the designs and attempts of *Great-Britain.*

" All wise states will well consider how to preserve the advantages arising from colonies, and avoid the evils. And I conceive that there can be but TWO ways in nature to hinder them from throwing off their dependence; *one* to keep it out of their *power*, and the *other*, out of their *will.* The first must be by *force*, and the *latter* by *using them well*, and keeping them employed in such productions, and making such manufactures, as will support themselves and families comfortably, *and procure them wealth too*, and at least not prejudice their mother country.

" *Force* can never be used effectually to answer the end, *without destroying the colonies themselves.* Liberty and encouragement are necessary to carry people thither, and to keep them together when they are there; and violence will hinder both. Any body of troops, considerable enough to awe them, and keep them in subjection, under the direction too of a needy governor, often sent thither to make his fortune, and at such a distance from any application for redress, will soon put an end to all planting, and leave the country to the soldiers alone, and if it did not, *would eat up all the profit of the colony.* For this reason, arbitrary countries have not been equally successful in planting colonies with free ones; and what they have done in that kind, has either been by force, or at a vast expence, or *by departing from the nature of their government*, and *giving such privileges to planters* as were *denied to their other subjects.* And I dare say, that a few prudent laws, and a little prudent conduct, would soon give us far the greatest share of the riches of all *America*, perhaps drive many of other nations out of it, or into other colonies for shelter

" There are *so many exigencies* in all states, *so many foreign wars*, and *domestic disturbances*, that these colonies CAN NEVER WANT OPPORTUNITIES, if they watch for them, *to do what they shall find their interest to do*; and therefore we ought to take all the precautions in our power, that it shall never be *their interest* to act against that of their native country, an evil which can no otherwise be averted, than by keeping them *fully employed* in such trades *as will increase their own*, as well as our wealth, for it is much to be feared, if we do not find employment for *them*, they may find it for *us*, the interest of the mother country, is always to keep them dependent, and so employed, and it requires all her address to do it, and it is certainly more *easily* and *effectually* done by *gentle* and *insensible* methods, than by *power* alone." CATO's *Letters*,

own children, which, if executed, muſt, in their opinion, ſink them into ſlaves : AND FOR WHAT ? For a
pernicious power, not neceſſary to her, as her own experience may convince her ; but horribly dreadful
and deteſtable to them.

IT ſeems extremely probable, that when cool, diſ-
paſſionate poſterity, ſhall conſider the affectionate in-
tercourſe, the reciprocal benefits, and the unſuſpecting
confidence, that have ſubſiſted between theſe colonies
and their parent country, for ſuch a length of time,
they will execrate, with the bittereſt curſes the infamous memory of thoſe men, whoſe peſtilential ambition
unneceſſarily, wantonly, cruelly, firſt opened the
ſources of civil diſcord between them ; firſt turned
their love into jealouſy ; and firſt taught theſe provinces, filled with grief and anxiety, to enquire---
　　　　　Mens ubi materna eſt ?
　　　　　Where is maternal affection ?

　　　　　　　A FARMER.

L E T.

LETTER VI.

My dear COUNTRYMEN,

IT may perhaps be objected against the arguments that have been offered to the public, concerning the legal power of the parliament, " that it has always exercised the power of imposing duties, for the purposes of raising a revenue on the productions of these colonies carried to *Great-Britain*, which may be called a tax on them." To this objection I answer, that this is no violation of the rights of the colonies, it being implied in the relation between them and *Great-Britain*, that they should not carry such commodities to other nations, as should enable them to interfere with the mother country. The imposition of duties on these commodities, when brought to her, is only a consequence of her parental right ; and if the point is thoroughly examined, the duties will be found to be laid on the people of the mother country. Whatever they are, they must proportionably raise the price of the goods, and consequently must be paid by the consumers. In this light they were considered by the parliament in the 25th *Charles* II. Chap. 7, Sect. 2, which says, that the productions of the plantations were carried from one to another free from all customs, " while the subjects of this your kingdom of *England* have paid *great customs and impositions for what of them have been* SPENT HERE," &c.

BESIDES, if *Great-Britain* exports these commodities again, the duties will injure her own trade, so that she cannot hurt us, without plainly and immediately hurting herself ; and this is our check against her acting arbitrarily in this respect.

* It

* It may be perhaps further objected, " that it being granted that ftatutes made for regulating trade, are binding upon us, it will be difficult for any perfon, but the makers of the laws, to determine, which of them are made for the regulating of trade, and which for raifing a revenue ; and that from hence may arife confufion,"

To this I anfwer, that the objection is of no force in the prefent cafe, or fuch as refemble it ; becaufe the act now in queftion, is formed *exprefly* FOR THE SOLE PURPOSE OF RAISING A REVENUE.

However, fuppofing the defign of parliament had not been *exprefjed*, the objection feems to me of no

F   weight,

---

* If any one fhould obferve that no oppofition has been made to the legality of the 4th *Geo.* III Chap 15, which is the FIRST act of parliament that ever impofed duties on the importations into *America*, for the *exprefed* purpofe of raifing a revenue there ; I anfwer, Firft, That tho' the act exprefly mentions the raifing a revenue in *America*, yet it feems that it had as much in view the " improving and fecuring the trade between the fame and *Great-Britain*," which words are part of its title . And the preamble fays, " Whereas it is expedient that new provifions and regulations fhould be eftablifhed for improving the revenue of this kingdom, and *for extending and fecuring the navigation and commerce between* Great-Britain, *and your Majefty's dominions in* America which by the peace have been fo happily extended and enlarged," *&c.* Secondly, *All* the duties mentioned in that act are impofed folely on the *productions and manufactures of foreign countries*, and not a fingle duty laid on any production or manufacture of our mother country. Thirdly, the authority of the provincial affemblies is not therein fo plainly *attacked* as by the laft act, which makes provifion for defraying the charges of the " adminiftration of juftice," and " the fupport of civil government " Fourthly, That it being *doubtful*, whether the intention of the 4th *Geo* III. Chap 15, was not as much *to regulate trade*, as *to raife a revenue*, the minds of the people here were wholly engroffed by the terror of the *Stamp-Act*, then impending over them, about the intention of which there could be no *doubt*.

Thefe reafons fo far diftinguifh the 4th *Geo* III Chap 15, from the laft act, that it is not to be wondered at, that the firft fhould have been fubmitted to, tho' the *laft* fhould excite the moft univerfal and fpirited oppofition For *this* will be found, on the ftricteft examination, to be, in the *principle* on which it is founded, and in the *confequences* that muft attend it, if poffible, more deftructive than the *Stamp-Act*. It is, to fpeak plainly, a *prodigy* in our laws , not having one *Britifh* feature.

weight, with regard to the influence which thofe who may make it, might expect it ought to have on the conduct of thefe colonies.

IT is true, that *impofitions for raifing a revenue*, may be hereafter called *regulations of trade*: But names will not change the nature of things. Indeed we ought firmly to believe, what is an undoubted truth, confirmed by the unhappy experience of many ftates heretofore free, that UNLESS THE MOST WATCHFUL ATTENTION BE EXERTED, A NEW SERVITUDE MAY BE SLIPPED UPON US, UNDER THE SANCTION OF USUAL AND RESPECTABLE TERMS.

THUS the *Cæfars* ruined the *Roman* liberty, under the titles of *tribunical* and *dictatorial* authorities, old and venerable dignities, known in the moft flourifhing times of freedom. In imitation of the fame policy, *James* II. when he *meant* to eftablifh popery, *talked* of liberty of confcience, the moft facred of all liberties; and had thereby almoft deceived the Diffenters into deftruction.

ALL artful rulers, who ftrive to extend their power beyond its juft limits, endeavor to give to their attempts as much femblance of legality as poffible. Thofe who fucceed them may venture to go a little further; for each new encroachment will be ftrengthened by a former. " † That which is now fupported by examples, growing old, will become an example itfelf," and thus fupport frefh ufurpations.

A FREE people therefore can never be too quick in obferving, nor too firm in oppofing the beginnings of *alteration* either in *form* or *reality*, refpecting inftitutions formed for their fecurity. The firft kind of alteration leads to the laft. Yet, on the other hand,
nothing

† TACITUS

nothing is more certain, than that the *forms* of liberty may be retained, when the *substance* is gone. In government, as well as in religion, " The *letter* killeth, but the *spirit* giveth life ‡."

I will beg leave to enforce this remark by a few instances. The crown, by the constitution, has the prerogative of creating peers. The existence of that order, in due number and dignity, is essential to the constitution; and if the crown did not exercise that prerogative, the peerage must have long since decreased so much as to have lost its proper influence. Suppose a prince, for some unjust purposes, should, from time to time, advance so many needy, profligate wretches to that rank, that all the independence of the house of lords should be destroyed; there would then be a manifest violation of the constitution, *under the appearance of using legal prerogative.*

The house of commons claim the privilege of forming all money bills, and will not suffer either of the other branches of the legislature to add to, or alter them; contending that their power simply extends to an acceptance or rejection of them. This privilege appears to be just: but under pretence of this just privilege, the house of commons has claimed a licence of tacking to money bills, clauses relating to things of a totally different kind, and thus forcing them in a manner on the king and lords. This seems to be an abuse of that privilege, and it may be vastly more abused. Suppose a future house, influenced by some displaced, discontented demagogues---in a time of danger, should tack to a money bill, something so injurious to the king and peers, that they would not assent to it, and yet the commons should obstinately insist on it; the whole kingdom would be exposed to ruin by them, *under the appearance of maintaining a valuable privilege.*

F 2
In

‡ 2 Cor. iii. 6.

IN thefe cafes it might be difficult for a while to determine, whether the king intended to exercife his prerogative in a conftitutional manner or not; or whether the commons infifted on their demand factioufly, or for the public good: But furely the conduct of the crown or of the houfe, would in time fufficiently explain itfelf.

OUGHT not the PEOPLE therefore to watch? to obferve facts? to fearch into caufes? to inveftigate defigns? And have they not a right of JUDGING from the evidence before them, on no flighter points than their *liberty* and *happinefs?* It would be lefs than trifling, wherever a *Britifh* government is eftablifhed, to make ufe of any arguments to prove fuch a right. It is fufficient to remind the reader of the day, on the anniverfary of which the firft of thefe letters is dated,

I WILL now apply what has been faid to the prefent queftion.

THE *nature* of any impofitions laid by parliament on thefe colonies, muft determine the *defign* in laying them. It may not be eafy in every inftance to difcover that defign. Wherever it is doubtful, I think fubmiffion cannot be dangerous; nay, it muft be right; for, in my opinion, there is no privilege thefe colonies claim, which they ought in *duty* and *prudence* more earneftly to maintain and defend, than the authority of the *Britifh* parliament to regulate the trade of all her dominions. Without this authority, the benefits fhe enjoys from our commerce, muft be loft to her: The bleffings we enjoy from our dependence upon her, muft be loft to us. Her ftrength muft decay; her glory vanifh; and fhe cannot fuffer without our partaking in her misfortune. *Let us therefore cherifh her interefts as our own, and give her every thing, that it becomes* FREEMEN *to give or to receive.*

THE

THE *nature* of any impofitions fhe may lay upon us may, in general, be known, by confidering how far they relate to the preferving, in due order, the connection between the feveral parts of the *Britifh* empire. One thing we may be affured of, which is this——Whenever fhe impofes duties on commodities, to be paid only upon their exportation from *Great-Britain* to thefe colonies, it is not a regulation of trade, but a defign to raife a revenue upon us. Other inftances may happen, which it may not be neceffary at prefent to dwell on. I hope thefe colonies will never, to their lateft exiftence, want underftanding fufficient to difcover the intentions of thofe who rule over them, nor the refolution neceffary for afferting their interefts. They will always have the fame rights, that all free ftates have, of judging when their privileges are invaded, and of ufing all prudent meafures for preferving them.

Quocirca vivite fortes,
Fortiaque adverfis opponite pectora rebus.

Wherefore keep up your fpirits, and gallantly oppofe this adverfe courfe of affairs.

A FARMER.

LET-

LETTER VII.

My dear COUNTRYMEN,

THIS letter is intended more particularly for such of you, whose employments in life may have prevented your attending to the confideration of fome points that are of great and public importance: For many fuch perfons there muft be even in thefe colonies, where the inhabitants in general are more intelligent than any other people whatever, as has been remarked by ftrangers, and it feems with reafon.

SOME of you, perhaps, filled, as I know your breafts are, with loyalty to our moft excellent Prince, and with love to our dear mother country, may feel yourfelves inclined, by the affections of your hearts, to approve every action of thofe whom you fo much venerate and efteem. A prejudice thus flowing from goodnefs of difpofition, is amiable indeed. I wifh it could be indulged without danger. Did I think this poffible, the error fhould have been adopted, and not oppofed by me. But in truth, all men are fubject to the frailties of nature; and therefore whatever regard we entertain for the *perfons* of thofe who govern us, we fhould always remember that their conduct, as *rulers*, may be influenced by human infirmities.

WHEN any laws, injurious to thefe colonies, are paffed, we cannot fuppofe, that any injury was intended us by his Majefty, or the Lords. For the affent of the crown and peers to laws, feems, as far as I am able to judge, to have been vefted in them, more for their own fecurity, than for any other purpofe. On the other hand, it is the particular bufinefs of the people, to enquire and difcover what regulations are ufeful for themfelves, and to digeft and prefent them in the form of bills, to the other orders, to have them enacted in-

to

to laws. Where these laws are to bind *themselves*, it may be expected, that the house of commons will very carefully consider them : But when they are making laws that are not designed to bind *themselves*, we cannot imagine that their deliberations will be as * cautious and scrupulous, as in their own case.

I AM

---

* Many remarkable instances might be produced of the extraordinary inattention with which bills of great importance, concerning these colonies, have passed in parliament ; which is owing, as it is supposed, to the bills being brought in by the persons who have points to carry, so artfully framed, that it is not easy for the members in general, in the haste of business, to discover their tendency

The following instances shew the truth of this remark. When Mr. *Greenville*, in the violence of reformation, formed the 4th Geo. III. Chap. 15th, for regulating the *American* trade, the word "*Ireland*" was dropt in the clause relating to our iron and lumber, so that we could send these articles to no part of *Europe*, but to *Great Britain*. This was so unreasonable a restriction, and so contrary to the sentiments of the legislature for many years before, that it is surprizing it should not have been taken notice of in the house However the bill passed into a law. But when the matter was explained, this restriction was taken off by a subsequent act. I cannot positively say how long after the taking off this restriction, as I have not the act, but I think, in less than 12 months, another act of parliament passed, in which the word "*Ireland*" was left out, just as it had been before. The matter being a second time explained, was a second time regulated.

Now if it be considered, that the omission mentioned struck off with ONE word SO VERY GREAT A PART OF OUR TRADE, it must appear *remarkable* ; and equally so is the method by which *Rice* became an enumerated commodity.

" The enumeration was obtained (says Mr [a] *Gee*) by one *Cole*, a Captain of a ship, employed by a company then trading to *Caroline*, for several ships going from *England* thither, and purchasing rice for *Portugal* prevented *the aforesaid Captain* of a loading. Upon his coming home, he possessed one Mr *Lowndes*, a member of parliament *(who was very frequently employed to prepare bills)* with an opinion, that carrying rice directly to *Portugal*, was a prejudice to the trade of *England*, and PRIVATELY got a clause into an act, to make it an enumerated commodity, *by which means he secured a freight to himself* BUT THE CONSEQUENCE PROVED A VAST LOSS TO THE NATION "

I find that this clause, " PRIVATELY got into an act," FOR THE BENEFIT OF CAPTAIN COLE, to the " VAST LOSS OF THE NATION," is foisted into the 3d and 4th *Ann*. Chap 5th, intituled, " An act for granting to her Majesty a further subsidy on wines and merchandizes imported," with which it has no more connection, than with 34th *Edward* I the 34th and 35th of *Henry* VIII. and the 25th of *Charles* II. WHICH PROVIDE, THAT NO PERSON SHALL BE TAXED BUT BY HIMSELF OR HIS REPRESENTATIVE

[a] *Gee* on Trade, page 32.

I AM told, that there is a wonderful address frequently used in carrying points in the house of commons, by persons experienced in these affairs.----That opportunities are watched---and sometimes votes are passed, that if all the members had been present, would have been rejected by a great majority. Certain it is, that when a powerful and artful man has determined on any measure against these colonies, he has always succeeded in his attempt. Perhaps therefore it will be proper for us, whenever any oppressive act affecting us is passed, to attribute it to the inattention of the members of the house of commons, and to the malevolence or ambition of some factious great man, rather than to any other cause.

Now I do verily believe, that the late act of parliament, imposing duties on paper, &c. was formed by Mr. *Greenville*, and his party, because it is evidently a part of that plan, by which he endeavoured to render himself POPULAR at home; and I do also believe, that not one half of the members of the house of commons, even of those who heard it read, did perceive how destructive it was to *American* freedom. For this reason as it is usual in *Great-Britain*, to consider the King's speech as the speech of the ministry, it may be right here to consider this act as the act of a *party*---perhaps I should speak more properly, if I was to use another term.

THERE are two ways of laying taxes. One is, by imposing a certain sum on particular kinds of property, to be paid by the *user* or *consumer*, or by rating the *person* at a certain sum. The other is, by imposing a certain sum on particular kinds of property, to be paid by the *seller*.

WHEN a man pays the first sort of tax, he *knows with certainty* that he pays so much money *for a tax.*

The

The *consideration* for which he pays it, i. remote; and, it may be, does not occur to him. He is sensible too, that he is *commanded and obliged* to pay it *as a tax*; and therefore people are apt to be displeased with this sort of tax.

The other sort of tax is submitted to in a very different manner. The purchaser of an article, very seldom reflects that the seller raises his price, so as to indemnify himself for the tax *he* has paid. He knows that the prices of things are continually fluctuating, and if he thinks about the tax, he thinks at the same time, in all probability, that he *might* have paid as much, if the article he buys had not been taxed. He gets something *visible* and *agreeable* for his money; and tax and price are so confounded together, that he cannot separate, or does not chuse to take the trouble of separating them.

This mode of taxation therefore is the mode suited to arbitrary and oppressive governments. The love of liberty is so natural to the human heart, that unfeeling tyrants think themselves obliged to accommodate their schemes as much as they can to the appearance of justice and reason, and to deceive those whom they resolve to destroy, or oppress, by presenting to them a miserable picture of freedom, when the inestimable original is lost.

This policy did not escape the cruel and rapacious *NERO.* That monster, apprehensive that his crimes might endanger his authority and life, thought proper to do some popular acts, to secure the obedience of his subjects. Among other things, says *Tacitus,* " he remitted the twenty fifth part of the price on the sale of slaves, but rather in *shew* than *reality*; for the *seller* being ordered to pay it, it became part of the price to the *buyer*†."

G

This

† *Tacitus's Ann.* Book 13, § 31.

THIS is the reflection of the judicious *Historian*; but the deluded *people* gave their intamous Emperor full credit for his false generofity. Other nations have been treated in the fame manner the *Romans* were. The honeft, induftrious *Germans*, who are fettled in different parts of this continent, can inform us, that it was this fort of tax that drove them from their native land to our woods, at that time the feats of perfect and undifturbed freedom.

THEIR Princes, enflamed by the luft of power, and the luft of avarice, two furies that the more they are gorged, the more hungry they grow, tranfgreffed the bounds they ought, in regard to themfelves, to have obferved. To keep up the deception in the minds of fubjects, " there muft be," fays ¶ a very learned author, " fome proportion between the impoft and the value of the commodity; wherefore there ought not to be an exceffive duty upon merchandizes of little value. There are countries in which the duty exceeds feventeen or eighteen times the value of the commodity. In this cafe the Prince removes the illufion. His fubjects plainly fee they are dealt with in an unreafonable manner, which renders them moft exquifitely fenfible of their flavifh fituation." From hence it appears, that fubjects may be ground down into mifery by this fort of taxation, as well as by the former. They will be as much impoverifhed, if their money is taken from them in this way as in the other; and that it will be taken, may be more evident, by attending to a few more confiderations.

THE merchant or importer, who pays the duty at firft, will not confent to be fo much money out of pocket. He therefore proportionably raifes the price of his goods. It may then be faid to be a conteft between
him

¶ *Montefquieu's Spirit of Laws,* Book 13, Chap. 8.

him and the person offering to buy, who shall lose the duty. This must be decided by the nature of the commodities, and the purchaser's demand for them. If they are mere luxuries, he is at liberty to do as he pleases, and if he buys, he does it voluntarily: But if they are absolute *neceffaries* or *conveniencies*, which use and custom have made requisite for the comfort of life, and which he is not permitted, by the power imposing the duty, *to get elfewhere*, there the seller has a plain advantage, and the buyer *must* pay the duty. In fact, the seller is nothing-less than a collector of the tax for the power that imposed it. If these duties then are extended to the necessaries and conveniencies of life in general, and enormously encreased, the people must at length become indeed " most exquifitely fenfible of their flavish fituation." Their happinefs therefore entirely depends on the moderation of those who have authority to impose the duties.

I SHALL now apply these observations to the late act of parliament. Certain duties are thereby imposed on paper and glafs, imported into these colonies. By the laws of *Great-Britain* we are prohibited to get these articles from any other part of the world. We cannot at present, nor for many years to come, tho' we should apply ourselves to these manufactures with the utmost industry, make enough ourselves for our own use. That paper and glafs are not only convenient, but absolutely neceffary for us, I imagine very few will contend. Some perhaps, who think mankind grew wicked and luxurious, as soon as they found out another way of communicating their fentiments than by speech, and another way of dwelling than in caves, may advance fo whimfical an opinion. But I presume no body will take the unneceffary trouble of refuting them.

FROM these remarks I think it evident, that we *must* use paper and glafs ; that what we use *must* be

G 2   *Britifh*

British; and that we *muft* pay the duties impofed, un-lefs thofe who fell thefe articles, are fo generous as to make us prefents of the duties they pay.

SOME perfons may think this act of no confequence, becaufe the duties are fo *fmall*. A fatal error. *That* is the very circumftance moft alarming to me. For I am convinced, that the authors of this law would never have obtained an act to raife fo trifling a fum as it muft do, had they not intended by *it* to eftablifh a *precedent* for future ufe. To confole ourfelves with the *fmallnefs* of the duties, is to walk deliberately into the fnare that is fet for us, praifing the *neatnefs* of the workmanfhip. Suppofe the duties impofed by the late act could be paid by thefe diftreffed colonies with the utmoft eafe, and that the purpofes to which they are to be applied, were the moft reafonable and equitable that can be con-ceived, the contrary of which I hope to demonftrate before thefe letters are concluded ; yet even in fuch a fuppofed cafe, thefe colonies ought to regard the act with abhorrence. For WHO ARE A FREE PEOPLE ? Not *thofe*, over whom government is reafonably and equitably exercifed, but *thofe*, who live under a go-vernment fo *conftitutionally checked* and *controuled*, that proper provifion is made againft its being otherwife exercifed.

THE late act is founded on the deftruction of this conftitutional fecurity. If the parliament have a right to lay a duty of Four Shillings and Eight-pence on a hundred weight of glafs, or a ream of paper, they have a right to lay a duty of any other fum on either. They may raife the duty, as the author before quoted fays has been done in fome countries, till it " exceeds feven-teen or eighteen times the value of the commodity." In fhort, if they have a right *to* levy a tax of *one penny* upon us, they have a right to levy a *million* upon us : For where does their right ftop ? At any given number of Pence, Shillings or Pounds ? To attempt to limit their

their right, after granting it to exist at all, is as contrary to reason----as granting it to exist at all, is contrary to justice. If *they* have any right to tax *us*----then, whether *our own money* shall continue in *our own pockets* or not, depends no longer on *us*, but on *them*. † " There is nothing which" we " can call our own ; or, to use the words of Mr. *Locke*----WHAT PROPERTY HAVE" WE " IN THAT, WHICH ANOTHER MAY, BY RIGHT, TAKE, WHEN HE PLEASES, TO HIMSELF ?"

THESE duties, which will inevitably be levied upon us---which are now levying upon us---are *expresly* laid FOR THE SOLE PURPOSES OF TAKING MONEY. This is the true definition of "*taxes.*" They are therefore *taxes.* This money is to be taken from *us. We* are therefore *taxed. Those* who are *taxed* without their own consent, expressed by themselves or their representatives, are *slaves. We are taxed* without our own consent, expressed by ourselves or our representatives. *We* are therefore--- * SLAVES.

'Miserable vulgus
A miserable tribe.

A FARMER.

† Lord *Cambden's* speech.

* " It is my opinion, that this kingdom has no right to lay A TAX upon the colonies."---" The *Americans* are the SONS, not the BASTARDS of *England*."---" The distinction between LEGISLATION and TAXATION is essentially necessary to liberty."---" The COMMONS of *America*, represented in their several assemblies, have ever been in possession of this their constitutional right, of GIVING AND GRANTING THEIR OWN MONEY They would have been *SLAVES,* if they had not enjoyed it." " The idea of a *virtual representation* of *America* in this house, is the most contemptible idea, that ever entered into the head of man.--- It does not deserve a serious refutation "

Mr. Pitt's *speech on the* Stamp-Act.

That great and excellent man Lord *Cambden,* maintains the same opinion. His speech in the house of peers, on the declaratory bill of the sovereignty of *Great-Britain* over the colonies, has lately appeared in our papers. The following extracts so perfectly agree with, and confirm the sentiments avowed in these letters, that it is hoped the inserting them in this note will be excused

" As the Affair is of the *utmost importance*, and in its consequences may involve the *fate of kingdoms*, I took the strictest review of my arguments,

LETTER VIII.

My dear COUNTRYMEN,

IN my opinion, a dangerous example is set in the last act relating to these colonies. The power of parliament to levy money upon us for raising a revenue, is therein *avowed* and *exerted*. Regarding the act on this single principle, I must again repeat, and I think it my duty to repeat, that to me it appears to be *un-constitutional.*

No

guments, I re examined all my authorities, fully determined if I found my self mistaken, publickly to own my mistake, and give up my opinion. But my searches have more and more convinced me that the *British* parliament have NO RIGHT TO TAX the *Americans*. "Nor is the doctrine new, it is as old as the the constitution; it grew up with it; indeed it is its support — " TAXATION and REPRESENTATION are inseparably united. GOD hath joined them. No *British* parliament can seperate them. To endeavour to do it, is to stab our vitals."

" My position is this — I repeat it, I will maintain it to my last hour — TAXATION and REPRESENTATION are inseparable — his position is founded on the laws of nature, it is more, it is itself AN ETERNAL LAW OF NATURE, for whatever is a man's own, is absolutely his own; NO MAN HATH A RIGHT TO TAKE IT FROM HIM WITHOUT HIS CONSENT, either expressed by himself or representative, *whoever attempts to do it, attempts an injury*, WHOEVER DOES IT COMMITS A ROBBERY, HE THROWS DOWN THE DISTINCTION BETWEEN LIBERTY AND SLAVERY." — " There is not a *blade of grass*, in the most obscure corner of the kingdom, which is not, which was n t ever *represented*, since the constitution began. There is not a *blade of grass*, which when taxed, *is not taxed by the consent of the proprietor*." " The forefathers of the *Americans* did not leave their native country, and subject themselves to every danger and distress, TO BE REDUCED TO A STATE OF SLAVERY. They did not give up their rights. They looked for protection, and *not for* CHAINS, from their mother country. By her they expected to be defended in the possession of their property, and not to be deprived of it. For should the present power continue, THERE IS NOTHING WHICH THEY CAN CALL THEIR OWN, or to use the words of Mr *Locke*, " WHAT PROPERTY HAVE THEY IN THAT, WHICH ANOTHER MAY, BY RIGHT, TAKE, WHEN HE PLEASES, TO HIMSELF?"

It is impossible to read this speech, and Mr *Pitt's*, and not be charmed with the generous zeal for the rights of mankind that glows in every sentence. These great and good men, animated by the subject they speak upon, seem to rise above all the former glorious exertions of their abilities. A foreigner might be tempted to think they are *Americans* asserting with all the ardor of patriotism, and all the anxiety of apprehension, the cause of their native land — and not *Britons*, striving to keep their mistaken country men from oppressing others. Their reasoning is not only just — it is, as Mr *Hume* says of the eloquence of *Demosthene*, " vehement." It is disdain, anger, boldness, freedom, involved in a continual stream of argument.

No man, who confiders the conduct of the parliament fince the repeal of the *Stamp-Act*, and the difpofition of many people at home, can doubt, that the
chief object of attention there, is, to ufe Mr *Greenville*'s expreffion, " providing that the DEPENDENCE
and OBEDIEN E of the colonies be afferted and maintained."

UNDER the influence of this notion, inftantly on
repealing the *Stamp-Act*, an act paffed, declaring the
power of parliament to bind thefe colonies *in all cafes
whatever*. This however was only planting a barren
tree, that caft a *fhade* indeed over the colonies, but
yielded no *fruit*   It being determined to enforce the
authority on which the *Stamp-Act* was founded, the
parliament having never renounced the right, as Mr.
Pitt advifed them to do , and it being thought proper
to difguife that authority in fuch a manner, as not
again to alarm the colonies · fome little time was re-
quired to find a method, by which both thefe points
fhould be united   At laft the ingenuity of Mr *Greenville* and his party accomplifhed the marter, as it was
thought, in " an act for granting certain duties in the
Britifh colonies and plantations in *America*, for allowing drawbacks," *&c* which is the title of the act laying
duties on paper, *&c.*

THE parliament having feveral times before impofed
duties to be paid in *America*, IT WAS EXPECTED, NO
DOUBT, THAT THE REPETITION OF SUCH A MEASURE
WOULD BE PASSED OVER, AS AN USUAL THING But
to have done this, without exprefly " afferting and
maintaining" the power of parliament to take our
money without our confent, and to apply it as they
pleafe, would not have been, in Mr. *Greenville*'s opinion, fufficiently declarative of its fupremacy, nor
fufficiently depreffive of *American* freedom.

THEREFORE

THEREFORE it is, that in this memorable act we find it *expresly* " provided," that money shall be levied upon us without our consent, for PURPOSES, that render it *if possible*, more dreadful than the *Stamp-Act*.

THAT act, alarming as it was, declared, the money thereby to be raised, should be applied " towards defraying the expences of defending, protecting and securing the *British* colonies and plantations in *America* :" And it is evident from the whole act, that by the word " *British*," were intended colonies and plantations *settled by* British *people*, and not generally, *those subject to the* British *crown*. That act therefore seemed to have something gentle and kind in its intention, and to aim only at *our own welfare* : But the act now objected to, impose duties upon the *British* colonies, " to defray the expences of defending, protecting and securing *his Majesty's* DOMINIONS *in* America."

WHAT a *change* of words! What an *incomputable addition* to the expences intended by the *Stamp-Act* ! " *His Majesty's* DOMINIONS" comprehend not only *the* British *colonies*, but also *the conquered provinces of* Canada *and* Florida, *and the* British *garrisons of* Nova-Scotia ; for *these* do not deserve the name of *colonies*.

WHAT justice is there in making us pay for " defending, protecting and securing" THESE PLACES ? What benefit *can* WE, or *have* WE ever derived *from them* ? None of them was conquered *for* us ; nor will " be defended, protected or secured" *for* us.

IN fact, however advantageous the subduing or keeping any of these countries may be to *Great-Britain*, the acquisition is greatly injurious to these colonies. Our chief property consists in *lands*. These would have been of much greater value, if such prodigious additions had not been made to the *British* territories

on

on this continent. The natural increase of our own people, if confined within the colonies, would have raised the value still higher and higher every fifteen or twenty years : Besides we should have lived more compactly together, and have been therefore more able to resist any enemy. But now the inhabitants will be thinly scattered over an immense region, as those who want settlements, will chuse to make new ones, rather than pay great prices for old ones.

These are the consequences to the colonies, of the hearty assistance they gave to *Great-Britain* in the late war---a war *undertaken solely for her own benefit.* The objects of it were, the securing to herself the rich tracts of land on the back of these colonies, with the *Indian* trade ; and *Nova-Scotia,* with the fishery. *These and much more, has that kingdom gained ;* but the *inferior animals,* that hunted with the *lion,* have been amply rewarded for all the sweat and blood their loyalty cost them, by the honor of having sweated and bled in such company.

I will not go so far as to say, that *Canada* and *Nova-Scotia* are curbs on *New-England ;* the *chain of forts* through the back woods, on the *Middle Provinces ;* and *Florida,* on the *rest :* But I will venture to say, that if the products of *Canada, Nova-Scotia,* and *Florida,* deserve any consideration, the two first of them are only rivals of our Northern Colonies, and the other of our Southern.

It has been said, that without the conquest of these countries, the colonies could not have been " protected, defended, and secured." If that is true, it may with as much propriety be said, that *Great-Britain* could not have been " defended, protected, and secured," without that conquest : For the colo-

H

nies

nies are parts of her empire, which it *as much concerns her* as *them* to keep out of the hands of any other power.

But these colonies, when they were much weaker, defended themselves, before this Conquest was made; and could again do it, against any that might properly be called *their* Enemies. If *France* and *Spain* indeed should attack them, *as members of the* British *empire*, perhaps they might be distressed; but it would be in a *British* quarrel.

The largest account I have seen of the number of people in *Canada*, does not make them exceed 90,000. *Florida* can hardly be said to have any inhabitants. It is computed that there are in our colonies 3,000,000. *Our* force therefore must increase with a disproportion to the growth of *their* strength, that would render us very safe.

This being the state of the case, I cannot think it just that these colonies, labouring under so many misfortunes, should be loaded with *taxes*, to maintain countries, not only not useful, but hurtful to them. The support of *Canada* and *Florida* cost yearly, it is said, half a million sterling. From hence, we may make some guess of the load that is to be laid *upon* us; for we are not only to " defend, protect and secure" *them*, but also to make " an adequate provision for defraying the charge of the administration of justice, and the support of civil government, in such provinces where it shall be found necessary."

Not one of the provinces of *Canada*, *Nova-Scotia*, or *Florida*, has ever defrayed *these expences within itself*: And if the duties imposed by the last statute are collected, *all of them together*, according to the best information I can get, will not pay *one quarter as much as* Pennsylvania *alone*. So that the *British colonies* are to
be

be drained of the rewards of their labor, to cherish the
scorching fands of *Florida*, and the icy rocks of *Canada*
and *Nova-Scotia*, which never will return to us one
farthing that we fend to them.

GREAT BRITAIN----I mean the miniftry in *Great-
Britain*, has cantoned *Canada* and *Florida* out into *five*
or *fix* governments, and may form *as many more*. There
now are *fourteen* or *fifteen* regiments on this continent ;
and there foon may be as *many more*. To make " an
adequate provifion" FOR ALL THESE EXPENCES, is, no
doubt, to be the *inheritance* of the colonies.

CAN any man believe that the duties upon paper,
&c. are the *laft* that will be laid for thefe purpofes ?
It is in vain to hope, that becaufe it is imprudent to
lay duties on the exportation of manufactures from a
mother country to colonies, as it may promote manufactures among them, that this confideration will prevent fuch a meafure.

AMBITIOUS, artful men have made it popular, and
whatever injuftice or deftruction will attend it in the
opinion of the colonifts, at home it will be thought juft
and falutary *.

THE people of *Great-Britain* will be told, and have
been told, that *they* are finking under an immenfe
debt----that great part of this debt has been contracted
in defending the colonies---that *thefe* are fo ungrateful and undutiful, that they will not contribute one
mite to its payment---nor even to the fupport of the
army now kept up for their " defence and fecurity"
that they are rolling in wealth, and are of fo bold and
republican a fpirit, that they are aiming at indepen-
H 2   dence,

* " So *credulous*, as well as *obftinate*, are the people in believing
every thing, which flatters their *prevailing paffion*.
                              Hume's Hift of England

dence---that the only way to retain them in " obedience," is to keep a ſtrict watch over them, and to draw off part of their riches in *taxes*---and that every burden laid upon *them*, is taking off ſo much from *Great-Britain*.----Theſe aſſertions will be generally believed, and the people will be perſuaded that they cannot be too angry with their colonies, as that anger will be profitable to themſelves.

In truth, *Great-Britain* alone receives any benefit from *Canada*, *Nova-Scotia* and *Florida* ; and therefore ſhe alone ought to maintain them. The old maxim of the law is drawn from reaſon and juſtice, and never could be more properly applied, than in this caſe.

Qui ſentit commodum, ſentire debet et onus.

They who feel the benefit, ought to feel the burden.

A FARMER.

LETTER IX.

My dear COUNTRYMEN,

I HAVE made some observations on the PURPOSES for which money is to be levied upon us by the late act of parliament. I shall now offer to your con-sideration some further reflections on that subject. And, unless I am greatly mistaken, if these purposes are accomplished according to the *expressed* intention of the act, they will be found effectually to *supersede* that authority in our respective assemblies, which is essential to liberty. The question is not, whether some branches shall be lopt'off----The axe is laid to the root of the tree; and the whole body must infal-libly perish, if we remain idle spectators of the work.

No free people ever existed, or can ever exist, with-out keeping, to use a common, but strong expression, " the purse strings," in their own hands. Where this is the case, *they* have a *constitutional check* upon the ad-ministration, which may thereby be brought into order *without violence:* But where such a power is not lodged in the *people*, oppression proceeds uncontrouled in its career, till the governed, transported into rage, seek redress in the midst of blood and confusion.

THE elegant and ingenious Mr. *Hume*, speaking of the *Anglo Norman* government, says----Princes and Ministers were too ignorant, to be themselves sensible of the advantage attending an equitable administrati-on, and there was no established council or *assembly*, WHICH COULD PROTECT THE PEOPLE, and BY WITH-DRAWING SUPPLIES, regularly and PEACEABLY admo-nish the king of his duty, and ENSURE THE EXECU-TION OF THE LAWS."

THUS

Thus this great man, whose political reflections are so much admired, makes *this power* one of the foundations of liberty.

The *English* history abounds with instances, proving that *this* is the proper and successful way to obtain redress of grievances. How often have kings and ministers endeavoured to throw off this legal curb upon them, by attempting to raise money by a variety of inventions, under pretence of law, without having recourse to parliament? And how often have they been brought to reason, and peaceably obliged to do justice, by the exertion of this constitutional authority of the people, vested in their representatives?

The inhabitants of these colonies have, on numberless occasions, reaped the benefit of this authority *lodged in their assemblies.*

It has been for a long time, and now is, a constant instruction to all governors, *to obtain a* PERMANENT *support for the offices of government.* But as the author of " the administration of the colonies" says, " this order of the crown is generally, if not universally, rejected by the legislatures of the colonies."

They perfectly know *how much* their grievances would be regarded, if they had *no other* method of engaging attention, than by *complaining.* Those who rule, are extremely apt to think well of the constructions made by themselves in support of their own power *These* are frequently erroneous, and pernicious to to those they govern. Dry remonstrances, to shew that such constructions are wrong and oppressive, carry very little weight with them, in the opinions of persons who gratify their own inclinations in making these constructions. *They* CANNOT understand the reasoning that opposes *their* power and desires. But let it

it be made *their interest* to underſtand ſuch reaſoning---
and a *wonderful light* is inſtantly thrown upon the matter ; and then, rejected remonſtrances become as clear
as * " proofs of holy writ,"

THE three moſt important articles that our aſſemblies, or any legiſlatures can provide for, are, Firſt---
the defence of the ſociety : Secondly----the adminiſtration of juſtice : And Thirdly----the ſupport of civil
government.

NOTHING can properly regulate the expence of making proviſion for theſe occaſions, but the *neceſſities* of
the ſociety , its *abilities* ; the *conveniency* of the modes
of levying money in it ; the *manner* in which the laws
have been executed : and the *conduct* of the officers of
government : *All which* are circumſtances, that *cannot*
poſſibly be properly *known*, but by the ſociety itſelf ;
or if they ſhould be known, *will not* probably be properly *conſidered* but by that ſociety.

IF money be raiſed upon us by *others*, without our
conſent, for our " defence," thoſe who are the judges
in *levying* it, muſt alſo be the judges in *applying* it Of
conſequence the money *ſaid* to be taken from us for
our defence, *may be employed* to our injury. We may
be chained in by a line of fortifications----obliged to
pay for the building and maintaining them---and be
told, that they are for our defence. With what face
can we diſpute the fact, after having granted that thoſe
who *apply* the money, had a right to *levy* it ? For
ſurely, it is much eaſier for their wiſdom to underſtand
how to apply it in the beſt manner, than how to levy
it in the beſt manner. Beſides, the *right of levying*
is of infinitely more conſequence, than *that of applying*.
The people of *England*, who would burſt out into fury,
if the crown ſhould attempt to *levy* money by its own
authority,

authority, have always assigned to the crown the *application* of money.

As to " the administration of justice"---the judges ought, in a well regulated state, to be equally independent of the executive and legislative powers. Thus in *England*, judges hold their commissions from the crown " *during good behaviour*," and have salaries, suitable to their dignity, *settled* on them by parliament. The purity of the courts of law since this establishment, is a proof of the wisdom with which it was made.

But in these colonies, how fruitless has been every attempt to have judges appointed " *during good behavior ?*" Yet whoever considers the matter will soon perceive, that *such commissions* are beyond all comparison more necessary in these colonies, than they were in *England.*

The chief danger to the subject *there*, arose from the arbitrary *designs of the crown*, but *here*, the time may come, when we may have to contend with the *designs of the crown, and of a mighty kingdom.* What then must be our chance, when the laws of life and death are to be spoken by judges totally dependent on *that crown*, and *that kingdom*---sent over perhaps *from thence*---filled with *British prejudices*----and *backed by a* STANDING *army*---supported out of OUR OWN pockets, to " assert and maintain" OUR OWN " dependence and obedience."

But supposing that through the extreme lenity that will prevail in the government *through all future ages*, these colonies will never behold any thing like the campaign of chief justice *Jeffereys*, yet what innumerable acts of injustice may be committed, and how fatally may the principles of liberty be sapped, by a succession of judges *utterly independent of the people ?* Before
such

such judges the supple wretches, who chearfully join in avowing sentiments inconsistent with freedom, will always meet with smiles; while the honest and brave men, who disdain to sacrifice their native land to their own advantage, but on every occasion boldly vindicate her cause, will constantly be regarded with frowns.

THERE are two other considerations relating to this head, that deserve the most serious attention.

BY the late act, the officers of the customs are " impowered to enter into any HOUSE, warehouse, shop, cellar, or other place, in the *British* colonies or plantations in *America*, to search for or seize prohibited or unaccustomed goods," &c. on " writs granted by the superior or supreme court of justice, having jurisdiction within such colony or plantation respectively."

IF we only reflect, that the judges of these courts are to be *during pleasure*---that they are to have " *adequate provision*" made for them, which is to continue *during their complaisant behavior*---that they may be *strangers* to these colonies---what an engine of oppression may this authority be in such hands ?

I AM well aware, that writs of this kind may be granted at home, under the seal of the court of exchequer : But I know also, that the greatest asserters of the rights of *Englishmen* have always strenuously contended, that *such a power* was dangerous to freedom, and expressly contrary to the common law, which ever regarded a man's *house* as his castle, or a place of perfect security.

IF such power was in the least degree dangerous *there*, it must be utterly destructive to liberty *here*. For the people there have two securities against the undue exercise of this power by the crown, which are

I   wanting

wanting with us, if the late act takes place. In the first place, if any injustice is done *there*, the person injured may bring his action against the offender, and have it tried before INDEPENDENT JUDGES, who are * NO PARTIES IN COMMITTING THE INJURY. *Here* he must have it tried before DEPENDENT JUDGES, being the men WHO GRANTED THE WRIT.

To say, that the cause is to be tried by a jury, can never reconcile men who have any idea of freedom, to *such a power*. For we know that sheriffs in almost every colony on this continent, are totally dependent on the crown, and packing of juries has been frequently practised even in the capital of the *British* empire. Even if juries are well inclined, we have too many instances of the influence of over-bearing unjust judges upon them. The brave and wise men who accomplished the revolution, thought the *independency of judges* essential to freedom.

THE other security which the people have at home, but which we shall want here, is this.

IF this power is abused *there*, the parliament, the grand resource of the oppressed people, is ready to afford relief. Redress of grievances must precede grants of money. But what regard can *we* expect to have paid to our assemblies, when they will not hold even the puny privilege of *French* parliaments—that of registering, before they are put in execution, the edicts that take away our money.

The second consideration above hinted at, is this. There is a *confusion* in our laws, that is quite unknown in *Great-Britain*. As this cannot be described in a
more

* The writs for searching houses in *England*, are to be granted
" under the feal of the court of exchequer," according to the statute
—and that feal is kept by the chancellor of the exchequer.
4th *Inst. p.* 104.

more clear or exact manner, than has been done by the ingenious author of the history of *New-York*, I beg leave to use his words " The state of our laws opens a door to much controversy. The *uncertainty*, with respect to them, RENDERS PROPERTY PRECARIOUS, and GREATLY EXPOSES US TO THE ARBITRARY DECISION OF BAD JUDGES. The common law of *England* is generally received, together with such statutes as were enacted before we had a legislature of our own, but our courts EXERCISE A SOVEREIGN AUTHORITY, in determining *what parts of the common and statute law* ought to be extended · For it must be admitted, that the *difference of circumstances* necessarily requires us, in some cases *to* REJECT *the determination of both*. In many instances, they have also extended even acts of parliament, passed since we had a distinct legislature, *which is greatly adding to our confusion* The practice of our courts is no less *uncertain* than the law Some of the *English* rules are adopted, others rejected. Two things therefore seem to be ABSOLUTELY NECESSARY for the PUBLIC SECURITY First, the passing an act for settling the extent of the *English* laws. Secondly, that the courts ordain a general sett of rules for the regulation of the practice."

How easy it will be, under this " state of our laws," for an artful judge, to act in the most arbitrary manner, and yet cover his conduct under specious pretences; and how difficult it will be for the injured people to obtain relief; may be readily perceived We may take a voyage of 3000 miles to complain; and after the trouble and hazard we have undergone, we may be told, that the collection of the revenue, and maintenance of the prerogative, must not be discouraged--- and if the misbehavior is so gross as to admit of no justification, it may be said, that it was an error in judgment only, arising from the confusion of our laws, and the zeal of the King's servants to do their duty.

If

IF the commiffions of judges are *during the pleafure of the crown*, yet if their falaries are *during the pleafure of the people*, there will be *fome check* upon their conduct. Few men will confent to draw on themfelves the hatred and contempt of thofe among whom they live, for the empty honor of being judges. It is the fordid love of gain, that tempts men to turn their backs on virtue, and pay their homage where they ought not.

As to the third particular, " the fupport of civil government,"---few words will be fufficient. Every man of the leaft underftanding muft know, that the *executive* power may be exercifed in a manner fo dif-agreeable and harraffing to the people, that it is abfo-lutely requifite, that *they* fhould be enabled by the gentleft method which human policy has yet been in-genious enough to invent, that is, *by fhutting their hands*, to " ADMONISH" (as Mr. *Hume* fays) certain perfons " OF THEIR DUTY."

WHAT fhall we now think when, upon looking in-to the late act, we find the affemblies of thefe provinces thereby ftript of their authority *on thefe feveral heads?* The *declared* intention of the act is, " that a revenue fhould be raifed IN HIS MAJESTY's DOMINIONS IN AMERICA, for making a more certain and adequate provifion *for defraying the charge of* THE ADMINISTRA-TION OF JUSTICE, and *the fupport of* CIVIL GOVERN-MENT in fuch provinces where it fhall be found necef-fary, and *towards further defraying the expences of* DE-FENDING, PROTECTING AND SECURING THE SAID DOMINIONS."

LET the reader paufe here one moment---and reflect ---whether the colony in which *he* lives, has not made fuch " certain and adequate provifion" *for thefe pur-pofes*, as is *by the colony judged fuitable to its abilities, and all other circumftances.* Then let him reflect---whether

if

if this act takes place, money is not to be raised on *that
colony without its consent,* to make " provision" *for
these purposes,* which *it does not judge to be suitable to
its abilities, and all other circumstances.* Lastly, let him
reflect---whether the people of that country are not in
a state of the most abject slavery, *whose property may be
taken from them* under the notion of right, *when they
have refused to give it.*

FOR my part, I think I have good reason for vindi-
cating the honor of the assemblies on this continent,
by publicly afferting, that THEY *have made as* " cer-
*tain and adequate provision" for the purposes abovemention-
ed, as they ought to have made,* and that it should not
be presumed, that they will not do it hereafter   Why
then should *these most important trusts* be wrested out of
their hands ? Why should they not now be permitted to
enjoy that authority, which they have exercised from
the first settlement of these colonies ? Why should they
be scandalized by this innovation, when their respective
provinces are now, and will be, for several years, labouring under loads of debt, imposed on them for the
very purpose now spoken of ? Why should all the inhabitants of these colonies be, with the utmost indig-
nity, treated as a herd of despicable stupid wretches,
so utterly void of common sense, that they will not even
make " adequate provision" for the administration of
justice, and the support of civil government" among
them, or for their own " defence"---though without
such " provision" every people must inevitably be
overwhelmed with anarchy and destruction ? Is it pof-
sible to form an idea of a slavery more *compleat,* more
miserable, more *disgraceful,* than that of a people, where
justice is administered, government exercised, and a *standing army maintained,* AT THE EXPENCE OF THE PEOPLE,
and yet WITHOUT THE LEAST DEPENDENCE UPON
THEM ? If we can find no relief from this infamous
situation, it will be fortunate for us, if Mr. *Greenville,*

setting

setting his fertile fancy again at work, can, as by one exertion of it he has stript us of our *property* and *liberty*, by another deprive us of so much of our *understanding*; that, unconscious of what we *have been* or *are*, and ungoaded by tormenting reflections, we may bow down our necks, with all the stupid serenity of servitude, to any drudgery, which our lords and masters shall please to command.

WHEN the charges of the "administration of justice," the "support of civil government," and the expences of "defending, protecting and securing" us, are provided, for, I should be glad to know, upon *what occasions* the crown will ever call our assemblies together. Some few of them may meet of their own accord, by virtue of their charters. But what will they have to do, when they are met? To what shadows will they be reduced? The men, whose deliberations heretofore had an influence on every matter relating to the *liberty* and *happiness* of themselves and their constituents, and whose authority in domestic affairs at least, might well be compared to that of *Roman* senators, will *now* find their deliberations of no more consequence, than those of *constables*. They may *perhaps* be allowed to make laws *for the yoking of hogs*, or *the pounding of stray cattle*. Their influence will hardly be permitted to extend *so high*, as the *keeping roads in repair*, as *that business* may more properly be executed by those who receive the public cash.

ONE most memorable example in history is so applicable to the point now insisted on, that it will form a just conclusion of the observations that have been made.

SPAIN was once *free*. Their *Cortes* resembled our parliaments. No *money* could be raised on the subject, *without their consent*. One of their Kings having received

ceived

ceived a grant from them, to maintain a war againſt the *Moors,* deſired, that if the ſum which they had given, ſhould not be ſufficient, he might be allowed, *for that emergency only,* to raiſe more money *without aſſembling the Cortes.* The requeſt was violently oppoſed by the beſt and wiſeſt men in the aſſembly. It was, however, complied with by the votes of a majority; and this ſingle conceſſion was a PRECEDENT for other conceſſions of the like kind, until at laſt the crown obtained a general power of raiſing money, in caſes of neceſſity. From that period the *Cortes* ceaſed to be *uſeful,*---the *people* ceaſed to be *free.*

Venienti occurite morbo.

Oppoſe a diſeaſe at its beginning.

A FARMER.

L E T T E R X.

My dear COUNTRYMEN,

THE confequences, mentioned in the laft letter, will not be the utmoft limits of our *mifery* and *infamy*, if the late act is acknowledged to be binding upon us. We feel too fenfibly, that *any ministerial measures* * relating to thefe colonies, are foon carried fuccefsfully through the parliament. Certain prejudices operate there fo ftrongly againft us, that it may be juftly queftioned, whether *all* the provinces united, will ever be able effectually to call to an account before the parliament, any minifter who fhall abufe the power by the late act given to the crown in *America.* He may divide the fpoils torn from us in what manner he pleafes, *and we fhall have no way of making him responsible.* If he fhould order, that every *governor* fhall have a yearly falary of 5000 l. fterling ; every *chief justice* of 3000 l , every inferior officer in proportion ; and fhould then reward the moft profligate, ignorant, or needy dependents on himfelf or his friends, with places of the greateft truft, becaufe they were of the greateft profit, this would be called an arrangement in confequence of the " adequate provifion for de. fraying the charge of the adminiftration of juftice, and the fupport of the civil government :" And if the taxes fhould prove at any time infufficient to anfwer all the expences of the numberlefs offices, which minifters may pleafe to create, furely the members of the houfe of commons will be fo " *modeft*," as not to " contradict a minifter" who fhall tell them, it is become neceffary

---

* " The gentleman muft not wonder he was not contradicted, when, as *minifter*, he afferted the right of parliament to tax *America* I know not how it is, but there is a MODESTY in this houfe, *which does not chufe to contradict a minifter*. I wifh gentlemen would get the better of this *modefty* IF THEY DO NOT, PERHAPS THE COLLECTIVE BODY MAY BEGIN TO ABATE OF ITS RESPECT FOR THE REPRESENTATIVE."
Mr. Pitt *s Speech.*

ceffary to lay a new tax upon the colonies, for the laudable purposes of defraying the charges of the " administration of juftice, and fupport of civil government," among them Thus, in fact, we fhall be †
taxed by minifters. In fhort, it will be in their power
to fettle upon us any CIVIL, ECCLESIASTICAL, or MILITARY eftablifhment, which they choofe.

WE may perceive, by the example of *Ireland*, how
eager minifters are to feize upon any fettled revenue,
and apply it in fupporting their own power. Happy
are the men, and *happy the people, who grow wife by
the misfortunes of others.* Earneftly, my dear countrymen, do I befeech the author of all good gifts, that
you may grow wife in this manner ; and if I may be
allowed to take fuch a liberty, I beg leave to recommend to you in general, as the beft method of attaining this wifdom, diligently to ftudy the hiftories of
other countries. You will there find all the arts, that
can poffibly be practifed by cunning rulers, or falfe
patriots among yourfelves, fo fully delineated, that,
changing names, the account would ferve for your own
times.

IT is pretty well known on this continent, that
Ireland has, with a regular confiftency of injuftice, been
cruelly treated by minifters in the article of *penfions* ;
but there are fome alarming circumftances relating to
that fubject, which I wifh to have better known
among us.

K   The

† " Within this act *(ftatute de tallagio non concedendo)* are all new offices erected, with new fees, or old offices, with new fees, for that is a
tallage put upon the fubject, which cannot be done without common
affent by act of parliament. And this doth notably appear by a petition to parliament in anno 13 *H.* IV where the commons complain, that an office was erected for measurage of cloths and canvas,
with a new fee for the fame, by colour of the king's letter patents, and pray that thefe letters patents may be revoked, for that
the king could erect no offices with new fees to be taken of the people,
who may not fo be charged but by parliament "   *2d. Inf p.* 533.

* The revenue of the crown there arises principally from the Excise granted "*for pay of the army, and defraying other* PUBLIC *charges, in defence and preservation of the kingdom*"---from the tonage and additional poundage granted "*for protecting the trade of the kingdom at sea, and augmenting the* PUBLIC *revenue*"---from the hearth money granted----as a "PUBLIC *revenue, for* PUBLIC *charges and expences.*" There are some other branches of the revenue, concerning which there is not any *express* appropriation of them for PUBLIC *service,* but which were plainly *so intended.*

Of *these* branches of the revenue the crown is only *trustee* for the public. They are unalienable. They are inapplicable to any other purposes, but those for which they were established; and therefore are not *legally* chargeable with pensions.   THERE

---

* An enquiry into the legality of pensions on the *Irish* establishment, by *Alexander M'Aulay,* Esq, one of the King's council, &c.

Mr *M'Aulay* concludes his piece in the following beautiful manner.---" If any *pensions* have been obtained on that establishment, to SERVE THE CORRUPT PURPOSES OF AMBITIOUS MEN.--If his Majesty's revenues of *Ireland* have been employed in pensions, TO DEBAUCH HIS MAJESTY's SUBJECTS of both kingdoms.----If the treasure of *Ireland* has been expended in pensions, FOR CORRUPTING MEN OF THAT KINGDOM TO BETRAY THEIR COUNTRY; and men of the neighbouring kingdom to betray both ---If *Irish* pensions have been procured, TO SUPPORT GAMESTERS AND GAMING-HOUSES, promoting a vice which threatens national ruin.----If pensions have been purloined out of the national treasure of *Ireland,* under the MASK OF SALARIES ANNEXED TO PUBLIC OFFICES, USELESS TO THE NATION; newly invented, FOR THE PURPOSES OF CORRUPTION.----It *Ireland,* just beginning to recover from the devastations of massacre and rebellion, be obstructed in the progress of her cure, BY SWARMS OF PENSIONARY VULTURES PREYING ON HER VITALS.----If, by squandering the national substance of *Ireland,* in a LICENTIOUS, UNBOUNDED PROFUSION OF PENSIONS, instead of employing it in nourishing and improving her infant *agriculture, trade* and *manufactures,* or in *enlightning* and *reforming* her *poor, ignorant, deluded, miserable natives* (by nature most amiable, most valuable, most worthy of public attention)---If *by such abuse of the national substance, sloth* and *nastiness, cold* and *hunger, nakedness* and *wretchedness, popery, depopulation* and *barbarism,* still maintain their ground; *still deform a country abounding with all the riches of nature,* yet hitherto destined to beggary.----If SUCH PENSIONS be found on the *Irish* establishment; let such be cut off: And let the perfidious advisers, be branded with indelible characters of public infamy, adequate, if possible, to the dishonour of their crime."

THERE is another kind of revenue, which is a private revenue. This is not limited to any public uses; but the crown has the same property in it, that any person has in his estate. This does not amount, at the most, to *Fifteen Thousand Pounds* a year, probably not to *Seven*, and is the only revenue, that can be *legally* charged with pensions.

IF ministers were accustomed to regard the rights or happiness of the people, the pensions in *Ireland* would not exceed the sum just mentioned: But long since have they exceeded that limit; and in *December* 1765, a motion was made in the house of commons in that kingdom, to address his Majesty on the great increase of pensions on the *Irish* establishment, amounting to the sum of 158,685l.---in the last two years.

ATTEMPTS have been made to gloss over these gross encroachments, by this specious argument---" That expending a competent part of the PUBLIC REVENUE in pensions, from a principle of charity or generosity, adds to the dignity of the crown; and is *therefore* useful to the PUBLIC." To give this argument any weight, it must appear, that the pensions proceed from *charity* or *generosity* only"---and that it " adds to the dignity of the crown," *to act directly contrary to law*.---

FROM this conduct towards *Ireland*, in open violation of law, we may easily foresee what *we may expect*, when a minister will have the *whole revenue* of *America* in his own hands, to be disposed of at his own pleasure; For *all* the monies raised by the late act are to be " *applied* by virtue of warrants under the sign manual, countersigned by the high treasurer, or any three of the commissioners of the treasury." The " RESIDUE" indeed is to be " paid into the receipt of the exchequer, and to be disposed of by parliament." So that a minister will have nothing to do, but to take care, that there shall be no " residue," and he is superior to all controul.

BESIDES

BESIDES the burden of *penfions* in *Ireland*, which have enormoufly encreafed within thefe few years, almoft all the *offices* in that poor kingdom, have been, fince the commencement of the prefent century, and now are beftowed upon *ftrangers*. For tho' the merit of perfons born there, juftly raifes them to places of high truft when they go abroad, as all *Europe* can witnefs, yet he is an uncommonly lucky *Irifhman*, who can get a good poft *in his* NATIVE *country*.

WHEN I confider the * manner in which that ifland has been uniformly depreffed for fo many years paft,
with

* In *Charles* the Second's time, the houfe of commons, influenced by fome factious demagogues, were refolved to prohibit the importation of *Irifh* cattle into *England*. Among other arguments in favour of *Ireland* it was infifted---" That by cutting off almoft entirely the trade between the kingdoms, ALL THE NATURAL BANDS OF UNION WERE DISSOLVED, and nothing remained to keep the *Irifh* in their duty, but *force* and *violence*"

" The king (fays Mr. *Hume*, in his hiftory of *England*) was fo convinced of the juftnefs of thefe reafons, that he ufed all his intereft to oppofe the bill, and he openly declared, that he could not give his affent to it with a fafe confcience. But the commons were refolute in their purpofe."----" And the fpirit of TYRANNY, *of which* NATIONS *are as fufceptible as* INDIVIDUALS, had animated the *Englifh* extremely TO EXERT THEIR SUPERIORITY *over their dependent ftate* No affair could be conducted with greater violence, than this by the commons. They even went fo far in the preamble of the bill, as to declare the importation of *Irifh* cattle to be a NUSANCE By this expreffion they gave fcope to their *paffion*, and at the fame time *barred the king's prerogative*, by which he might think himfelf intituled to difpenfe with a law, SO FULL OF INJUSTICE AND BAD POLICY. The lords expunged the word, but as the king was fenfible that no fupply would be given by the commons, unlefs they were gratified in all their PREJUDICES, he was obliged both to employ his intereft with the peers, to make the bill pafs, and to give the royal affent to it. He could not, however, forbear expreffing his difpleafure, at the jealoufy entertained againft him, and at the intention which the commons difcovered, of retrenching his prerogative.

THIS LAW BROUGHT GREAT DISTRESS FOR SOME TIME UPON IRELAND, BUT IT HAS OCCASIONED THEIR APPLYING WITH GREATER INDUSTRY TO MANUFACTURES, AND HAS PROVED IN THE ISSUE BENEFICIAL TO THAT KINGDOM."

. Perhaps the *fame reafon* occafioned the " barring the king's prerogative" in the late act fufpending the legiflation of *New York*.

This we may be affured of, that WE are as dear to his *Majefty*, as the people of *Great Britain* are We are his *fubjects* as well as they, and
as

with this pernicious particularity *of their † parliament*
continuing as long as the crown pleases, I am aftonifhed to
obferve *fuch a love of liberty* ftill animating that LOYAL
and GENEROUS nation ; and nothing can rife higher my
idea of the INTEGRITY and ‡ PUBLIC SPIRIT of a
people, who have preferved the facred fire of freedom
from being extinguifhed, tho' the altar on which it
burnt, has been overturned.

                                                                   IN

as faithful fubjects, and his Majefty has given too many, too conftant
proofs of his piety and virtue, for any man to think it poffible, that *fuch
a prince* can make any unjuft diftinction between *fuch fubjects*. It makes
no difference to his Majefty, whether fupplies are raifed in *Great-Britain*, or *America*, but it makes *fome* difference to the commons of that
kingdom

To fpeak plainly as becomes an honeft man on fuch important occa-
fions, all our misfortunes are owing to a LUST OF POWER in men of
abilities and *influence*. This prompts them to feek POPULARITY by *ex-
pedients* profitable to themfelves, though ever fo deftructive to their
country

Such is the accurfed nature of lawlefs ambition, and yet---What
heart but melts at the thought !---Such falfe, deteftable PATRIOTS, in
every ftate, have led their blind, confiding country, fhouting their ap-
plaufes, into the jaws of *fome* ano *rum* May the wifdom and goodnefs of the people of *Great-Britain*, fave them from the ufual fate of
nations.

        " ---------MENTUM MORTALIA TANGUNT "

  † The *Irifh* parliament cont'nued 33 years, during all the late King's
reign. The prefent parliament there has continued from the beginning of this reign, and probably will continue till this reign ends

  ‡ I am informed, that within thefe few years, a petition was prefented to the houfe of commons, fetting forth, " that herrings were
imported into *Ireland* from fome foreign parts of the north fo cheap, as
to difcourage the *Britifh* herring fifhery, and therefore praying that
fome remedy might be applied in that behalf by parliament."

That upon this petition, the houfe came to a refolution, to impofe a
duty of Two Shillings fterling on every barrel of foreign herrings imported into *Ireland*, but afterwards dropt the affair, FOR FEAR OF
ENGAGING IN A DISPUTE WITH IRELAND ABOUT THE RIGHT, OF
TAXING HER.

  So much higher was the opinion, which the houfe entertained of the
fpirit of *Ireland*, than of that of thefe colonies.

I find, in the laft *Englifh* papers, that the refolution and firmnefs with
which the people of *Ireland* have lately afferted their freedom, have
been fo alarming in *Great-Britain*, that the Lord Lieutenant, in his
fpeech on the 20th of laft *October*, " recommended to that parliament,
that fuch provifion may be made for fecuring the judges in the enjoy-
ment of their *offices* and *appointments*, DURING THEIR GOOD BEHAVIOR,
as fhall be thought moft expedient "

What an important conceffion is thus obtained, by making demands
becoming freemen, with a courage and perfeverance becoming Freemen !

In the same manner shall we unquestionably be treated, as soon as the late taxes laid upon us, shall make posts in the "government," and the "administration of justice" *here*, worth the attention of persons of influence in *Great-Britain*. We know enough already to satisfy us of this truth. But this will not be the worst part of our case.

The *principals*, in all great offices, will reside in *England*, making some paltry allowance to deputies for doing the business *here*. Let any man consider what an exhausting drain this must be upon us, when ministers are possessed of the power of creating what posts they please, and of affixing to such posts what salaries they please, and he must be convinced how destructive the late act will be. The injured kingdom lately mentioned, can tell us the mischiefs of ABSENTEES; and we may perceive already the same disposition taking place with us. The government of *New-York* has been exercised by a deputy. That of *Virginia* is now held so; and we know of a number of secretary-ship, collector-ships, and other offices, held in the same manner.

True it is, that if the people of *Great-Britain* were not too much blinded by the passions, that have been artfully excited in their breasts, against their dutiful children the colonists, these considerations would be nearly as alarming to them as to us. The influence of the crown was thought by wise men, many years ago, too great by reason of the multitude of pensions and places bestowed by it. These have been vastly encreased since †, and perhaps it would be no difficult matter to prove that the people have decreased.

SURELY

---

† One of the reasons urged by that great and honest statesman, Sir *William Temple*, to *Charles* the Second, in his famous remonstrance, to dissuade him from aiming at arbitrary power, was, that the King "had few offices to bestow."

Hume's Hist. of *England*.

Pho'

SURELY therefore, those who wish the welfare of their country, ought seriously to reflect, what may be the consequence of such a new creation of offices, in the disposal of the crown. The *army*, the *administration of justice*, and the *civil government* here, with such salaries as the crown shall please to annex, will extend *ministerial influence* as much beyond its former bounds, as the late war did the *British* dominions.

BUT whatever the people of *Great-Britain* may think on this occasion, I hope the people of these colonies will unanimously join in this sentiment, that the late act of parliament is injurious to their liberty, and that this sentiment will unite them in a firm opposition to it, in the same manner as the dread of the *Stamp-Act* did.

SOME persons may imagine the sums to be raised by it, are but small, and therefore may be inclined to acquiesce under it. A conduct more dangerous to freedom, as before has been observed, can never be adopted. Nothing is wanted at home but a * PRECE-

DENT,

" Tho' the wings of prerogative have been clipt, the influence of the crown is greater than ever it was in any period of our history For when we consider in how many boroughs the government has the votes at command; when we consider the vast body of persons employed in the collection of the revenue, in every part of the kingdom, the inconceivable number of placemen, and candidates for places in the customs, in the excise, in the post-office, in the dock-yards, in the ordnance, in the salt-office, in the stamps, in the navy and victualling offices, and in a variety of other departments; when we consider again the extensive influence of the money corporations, subscription jobbers and contractors, the endless dependencies created by the obligations conferred on the bulk of the gentlemens families throughout the kingdom, who have relations preferred in our navy and numerous standing army, when I say, we consider how wide, how binding a dependence on the crown is created by the above enumerated particulars, and the great, the enormous weight and influence which the crown derives from this extensive dependence upon its favor and power, any lord in waiting, any lord of the bed-chamber, any man may be appointed minister."

A doctrine to this effect is said to have been the advice of L--- H---.
Late News Paper.

* " Here may be observed, that when any ancient law or custom of parliament is broken, and the crown possessed of a *precedent*, how diffi

cult

DENT, the force of which shall be established, by the tacit submission of the colonies. With what zeal was the statute erecting the post office, and another relating to the recovery of debts in *America*, urged and tortured, as *precedents* in support of the *Stamp-Act*, tho' wholly inapplicable. If the parliament succeeds in this attempt, other statutes will impose other duties. Instead of taxing ourselves, as we have been accustomed to do, from the first settlement of these provinces, all our usual taxes will be converted into parliamentary taxes on our importations; and thus the parliament will levy upon us such sums of money as they chuse to take, *without any other* LIMITATION, *than their* PLEASURE.

WE know how much labor and care have been bestowed by these colonies, in laying taxes in such a manner, that they should be most *easy* to the people, by being laid on the proper articles; most *equal*, by being proportioned to every man's circumstances; and *cheapest*, by the method directed for collecting them.

BUT *parliamentary taxes* will be laid on us, without any consideration, whether there is any *easier* mode. The *only point* regarded will be, the *certainty of levying the taxes*, and not the *convenience* of the people on whom they are to be levied; and therefore all statutes on this head will be such as will be most likely, according to the favorite phrase, " *to execute themselves.*"

TAXES in every free state have been, and ought to be, as exactly *proportioned as is possible to the abilities of those who are to pay them*. They cannot otherwise be *just*. Even a *Hottentot* would comprehend the *unrea-*

cult a thing it is to restore the subject again to his FORMER FREEDOM and SAFETY." 2d. Coke's Inst. p. 529

" It is not almost credible to foresee, when any maxim or fundamental law of this realm is altered (as elsewhere hath been observed) what dangerous inconvenience do follow." 4th Coke's Inst. p. 41.

fonableneſs of making a poor man pay as much for
"defending" the property of a rich man, as the rich
man pays himſelf.

LET any perſon look into the late act of parliament,
and he will immediately perceive, that the immenſe
eſtates of Lord *Fairfax*, Lord ‡ *Baltimore*, and our
Proprietaries, which are amongſt his Majeſty's other
"DOMINIONS" to be "defended, protected and ſecured" by the act, will not pay a *ſingle farthing* for the
duties thereby impoſed, except Lord *Fairfax* wants
ſome of his windows glazed; Lord *Baltimore* and our
Proprietaries are quite ſecure, as they live in *England*.

I MENTION theſe particular caſes, as ſtriking in-
ſtances how far the late act is a deviation from *that
principle of juſtice*, which has ſo conſtantly diſtinguiſhed
our own laws on this continent, and ought to be regarded in all laws.

THE third conſideration with our continental aſſemblies in laying taxes, has been the *method* of collecting
them. This has been done by a few officers, with
moderate allowances, under the inſpection of the re-
ſpective aſſemblies. *No more was raiſed from the ſubject,*
than was uſed for the intended purpoſes. But by the
late act, a miniſter may appoint *as many officers as he
pleaſes* for collecting the taxes; may aſſign them *what
ſalaries he thinks* "adequate;" and they are ſubject to
no inſpection but his own.

IN ſhort, if the late act of parliament takes effect,
theſe colonies muſt dwindle down into "COMMON
L   CORPORATIONS,"

† *Maryland* and *Pennſylvania* have been engaged in the warmeſt diſ-
putes, in order to obtain an equal and juſt taxation of their Proprie-
tors eſtates: But this late act of parliament does more for thoſe Pro-
prietors, than they themſelves would venture to demand. It *totally
exempts* them from taxation--------tho' their vaſt eſtates are to be
"ſecured" by the taxes of other people.

CORPORATIONS," as their enemies, in the debates con‑
cerning the repeal of the *Stamp-Act, strenuously insisted
they were* ; and it seems not improbable that some
future historian may thus record our fall.

" THE eighth year of this reign was distinguished
by *a very memorable event*, the *American* colonies then
submitting, for the *FIRST* time, to be *taxed* by the
British parliament. An attempt of this kind had been
made about two years before, but was defeated by the
vigorous exertions of the several provinces, in defence
of their liberty. Their behavior on that occasion ren‑
dered their name very celebrated *for a short time* all over
Europe ; all states being extremely attentive to a dis‑
pute between *Great-Britain*, and so considerable a part
of her dominions. For as she was thought to be grown
too powerful, by the successful conclusion of the late
war she had been engaged in, it was hoped by many,
that as it had happened before to other kingdoms,
civil discords would afford opportunities of revenging
all the injuries supposed to be received from her. How‑
ever, the cause of dissention was removed, by a repeal
of the statute that had given offence. This affair ren‑
dered the SUBMISSIVE CONDUCT of the colonies so soon
after, the more extraordinary ; there being *no difference*
between the mode of taxation which they opposed, and
that to which they submitted, but this, that by the
first, they were to be continually *reminded* that they
were taxed, by certain marks *stamped* on every piece of
paper or parchment they used. The authors of *that
statute* triumphed greatly on this conduct of the colo‑
nies, and insisted, that if the people of *Great-Britain*
had persisted in enforcing it, the *Americans* would have
been, in a few months, *so fatigued with the efforts of pa‑
triotism*, that they would have yielded obedience.

" CERTAIN it is, that tho' they had before their
eyes *so many illustrious examples* in their mother country,
of

of *the constant success* attending *firmness* and *perseverance*, in oppofition to dangerous encroachments on liberty, yet they quietly gave up a point of the LAST IMPORT-ANCE. From thence the decline of their freedom began, and its decay was extremely rapid; for as *money* was always raised upon them by the parliament, their *affemblies* grew immediately *useless*, and in a fhort time *contemptible :* And in lefs than one hundred years, the people funk down into that *tamenefs* and *fupinenefs* of fpirit, by which they ftill continue to be diftinguifhed."

Et majores veftros & pofteros cogitate.

Remember your anceftors and your pofterity.

A FARMER.

L E T-

LETTER XI.

My dear COUNTRYMEN,

I HAVE several times, in the course of these letters, mentioned the late act of parliament, as
being the *foundation* of future measures injurious to
these colonies ; and the belief of this truth I wish to
prevail, because I think it necessary to our safety.

A PERPETUAL *jealousy*, respecting liberty, is absolutely requisite in all free-states. The very texture of
their constitution, in *mixt* governments, demands it.
For the *cautions* with which power is *distributed* among
the several orders, *imply*, that *each* has that share which
is proper for the general welfare, and therefore that
any further acquisition must be pernicious. * *Machiavel* employs a whole chapter in his discourses, to prove
that a state, to be long lived, must be frequently corrected, and reduced to its first principles. But of all
states that have existed, there never was any, in which
this jealousy could be more proper than in these colonies. For the government here is not only *mixt*, but
dependent, which circumstance occasions *a peculiarity in
its form*, of a very delicate nature.

Two reasons induce me to desire, that this spirit of
apprehension may be always kept up among us, in its
utmost vigilance. The first is this---that as the happiness of these provinces indubitably consists in their
connection with *Great-Britain*, any separation between
them is less likely to be occasioned by civil discords,
if every disgusting measure is opposed *singly*, and *while
it is new :* For in this manner of proceeding, every
such measure is most likely to be rectified. On the
other hand, oppressions and dissatisfactions being permitted to accumulate---*if ever* the governed throw off
the

* *Machiavel's Discourses---Book 3. Cap. 1.*

the load, *they will do no more*. A people does not re-
form with moderation. The rights of the fubject
therefore cannot be *too often* confidered, explained or
afferted : And whoever attempts to do this, fhews
himfelf, whatever may be the rafh and peevifh reflections of pretended wifdom, and pretended duty, a
friend to *thofe* who injudicioufly exercife their power,
as well as to *them*, over whom it is fo exercifed.

Had all the points of prerogative claimed by
Charles the Firft, been feparately contefted and fettled
in preceding reigns, his fate would in all probability
have been very different ; and the people would have
been content with that liberty which is compatible
with regal authority. But † he thought, it would be
as dangerous for him to give up the powers which at
any time had been by ufurpation exercifed by the
crown, as thofe that were legally vefted in it. This
produced an equal excefs on the part of the people.
For when their paffions were excited by *multiplied* grievances, they thought it would be as dangerous for
them to allow the powers that were legally vefted in
the crown, as thofe which at any time had been by
ufurpation exercifed by it. Acts, that might *by themfelves* have been upon many confiderations excufed or
extenuated, derived a contagious malignancy and odi-
-um from other acts, with which they were connected.
They were not regarded according to the fimple force
of each, but as parts of a fyftem of oppreffion. Every
one therefore, however fmall in itfelf, became alarming, as an additional evidence of tyrannical defigns.

It

---

† The author is fenfible, that this is putting the gentleft conftruction
on *Charles*'s conduct; and that is one reafon why he chooſes it. Allowances ought to be made for the errors of thofe men, who are acknowledged to have been poffeffed of many virtues. The education of this
unhappy prince, and his confidence in men not fo good or wife as himfelf, had probably *filled* him with miftaken notions of his own authority, and of the confequences that would attend conceffions of any kind
to a people, who were reprefented to him, as aiming at too much
power.

It was in vain for prudent and moderate men to infift, that there was no neceffity to abolifh royalty. Nothing lefs than the utter deftruction of monarchy, could fatisfy thofe who *had* fuffered, and thought they had reafon to believe, they always *fhould* fuffer under it.

THE confequences of thefe mutual diftrufts are well known : But there is no other people mentioned in hiftory, that I recollect, who have been fo conftantly watchful of their liberty, and fo fuccefsful in their ftruggles for it, as the *Englifh*. This confideration leads me to the fecond reafon, why I " defire that the fpirit of apprehenfion may be always kept up among us in its utmoft vigilance."

THE firft principles of government are to be looked for in human nature. Some of the beft writers have afferted, and it feems with good reafon, that " government is founded on * *opinion*."

CUSTOM undoubtedly has a mighty force in próducing *opinion*, and reigns in nothing more arbitrarily than in public affairs. It gradually reconciles us to objects even of dread and deteftation ; and I cannot but think thefe lines of Mr. *Pope* as applicable to vice in *politics*, as to vice in *ethics*——

 " Vice is a monfter of fo horrid mien,
 " As to be hated, needs but to be feen ;
 " Yet *feen too oft*, familiar with her face,
 " We firft *endure*, then *pity*, then *embrace*."

When

---

* " OPINION is of two kinds, *viz.* *opinion* of INTEREST, and *opinion* of RIGHT. By *opinion* of *intereft*, I chiefly underftand, *the fenfe of the public advantage which is reaped from government* ; together with the perfuafion, that the particular government which is eftablifhed, is *equally advantageous* with any other, *that could be eafily fettled* "
" *Right* is of two kinds, *right* to *power*, and *right* to *property*. What prevalence *opinion* of the firft kind has over mankind, may eafily be underftood, by obferving the attachment which all nations have to their antient government, and even to thofe names which have had the fanction of antiquity. *Antiquity always begets the opinion of right*."——
" It is fufficiently underftood, that the *opinion* of *right* to *property*, is of the greateft moment in all matters of government." *Hume's Effays*.

When an act injurious to freedom has been *once done*, and the people *bear* it, the *repetition* of it is most likely to meet with *submission*. For as the *mischief* of the one was found to be tolerable, they will hope that of the second will prove so too ; and they will not regard the *infamy* of the last, because they are stained with that of the first.

Indeed nations, in general, are not apt to *think* until they *feel* ; and therefore nations in general have lost their liberty : For as violations of the rights of the *governed*, are commonly not only ‡ *specious*, but *small* at the beginning, they spread over the multitude in such a manner, as to touch individuals but slightly. † Thus they are disregarded. The power or profit that arises from these violations, *centering in few persons*, is to them considerable. For this reason the *governors* having in view their particular purposes, successively preserve an uniformity of conduct for attaining them. They regularly encrease the first injuries, till at length the inattentive people are compelled to perceive the heaviness of their burthens.---They begin to complain and enquire---but too late. They find their oppressors so strengthened by success, and themselves so entangled in examples of express authority on the part of their rulers, and of tacit recognition on their own part, that

they

---

‡ Omnia mala exempla ex bonis initiis orta sunt.

Sallust *Bell Cat S.* 50

† " The *republic* is always *attacked* with greater vigor, than it is *defended*? For the *audacious* and *profligate*, prompted by their natural enmity to it, are *easily impelled* to act by the *least nod* of their *leaders* Whereas the honest, I know not why, are generally *slow* and *unwilling* to stir, and *neglecting* always the BEGINNINGS *of things*, are *never roused* to exert themselves, but by the *last necessity* So that through IRRESOLUTION and DELAY, when they would be glad to compound at last for their QUIET, at the expence even of their HONOR, they *commonly lose them* BOTH." CICERO's *Orat for* SEXTIUS.

Such were the sentiments of this great and excellent man, whose vast abilities, and the calamities of his country during his time, enabled him, by mournful experience, to form a just judgment on the conduct of the friends and enemies of liberty.

they are quite confounded : For millions entertain no other idea of the *legality* of power, than that it is founded on the *exercise* of power. They voluntarily fasten their chains, by adopting a pusil'animous *opinion,* " that there will be too much *danger* in attemping a remedy,".--or another *opinion* no lefs fatal,---" that the government has a *right* to treat them as it does." They then feek a wretched relief for their minds, by perfuading themfelves, that to yield their *obedience,* is to difcharge their *duty.* The deplorable *poverty of spirit,* that proftrates all the dignity beftowed by Divine Providence on our nature---*of courfe fucceeds.*

From thefe reflections I conclude, that every free ftate fhould inceffantly watch, and inftantly take alarm on any addition being made to the power exercifed over them. Innumerable inftances might be produced to fhew, from what flight beginnings the moft extenfive confequences have flowed : But I fhall felect two only from the hiftory of *England.*

Henry the Seventh was the *first* monarch of that kingdom, who eftablifhed a STANDING BODY OF ARMED MEN. This was a band of *fifty* archers, called yeomen of the guard : And this inftitution, notwithftanding the fmallnefs of the number, was, to prevent difcontent, * " difguifed under pretence of majefty and grandeur." In 1684 the ftanding forces were fo much augmented, that *Rapin* fays----" The king, in order to make his people *fully fensible of their new slavery,* affected to mufter his troops, which amounted to 4000 well armed and difciplined men " I think our army, at this time, confifts of more than *seventy* regiments.

The method of taxing by EXCISE was firft introduced amidft the convulfions of the civil wars. Extreme neceffity was pretended for it, and its fhort continuance

tinuance

* *Rapin*'s Hiftory of *England.*

tinuance promised. After the restoration, an excise upon *beer*, *ale* and *other liquors*, was granted to the * king, one half in fee, the other for life, as an equivalent for the *court of wards*. Upon *James* the Second's accession, the parliament ‡ gave him the first *excise*, with an additional duty on *wine*, *tobacco*, and some *other* things. Since the revolution it has been extended to salt, candles, leather, hides, hops, soap, paper, paste-boards, mill-boards, scale-boards, vellum, parchment, starch, silks, calicoes, linens, stuffs, printed, stained, &c. wire, wrought plate, coffee, tea, chocolate, &c.

THUS a *standing army* and *excise* have, from their first slender origins, tho' always *hated*, always *feared*, always *opposed*, at length swelled up to their vast present bulk.

THESE facts are sufficient to support what I have said. 'Tis true, that all the mischiefs apprehended by our ancestors from a *standing army* and *excise*, have not *yet happened*: But it does not follow from thence, that they *will not happen*. The inside of a house may catch fire, and the most valuable apartments be ruined, before the flames burst out. The question in these cases is not, what evil *has actually attended* particular measures---but, what evil, in the nature of things, *is likely to attend* them. Certain circumstances may for some time delay effects, that *were reasonably expected*, and that *must ensue*. There was a long period, after the *Romans* had prorogued his command to § *Q. Publilius Philo*,

M   before

---

* 12 *Char*. II. Chap. 23 and 24.
‡ 1 *James* II. Chap. 1 and 4.
§ In the year of the city 428, "Duo singularia hæc ei viro primum contingere; prorogatio imperii non ante in ullo facta et acto honore triumphus." *Liv*. B. 8. *Chap.* 23 26.
"Had the rest of the *Roman* citizens imitated the example of *L. Quintius*, who refused to have his consulship continued to him, they had never admitted that custom of proroguing of magistrates, and then the prolongation of their commands in the army had never been introduced, *which very thing was at length the ruin of that common wealth.*" *Machiavel's Discourses*, B. 3 *Chap.* 24.

before *that example* deſtroyed their liberty. All our kings, from the revolution to the preſent reign, have been *foreigners*. Their *miniſters* generally continued but a ſhort time in authority † ; and they themſelves were *mild* and *virtuous* princes.

A BOLD, *ambitious* prince, poſſeſſed of *great abilities*, firmly *fixed* in his throne *by deſcent*, ſerved by *miniſters like himſelf*, and rendered either *venerable* or *terrible* by the *glory of his ſucceſſes*, may execute what his pre-deceſſors did not dare to attempt. *Henry* the Fourth tottered in his ſeat during his whole reign. *Henry* the Fifth drew the ſtrength of that kingdom into *France*, to carry on his wars there, and left the *commons* at home, *proteſting*, " that the people were not bound to ſerve out of the realm."

IT is true, that a ſtrong ſpirit of liberty ſubſiſts at preſent in *Great-Britain*, but what reliance is to be placed in the *temper* of a people, when the prince is poſſeſſed of an unconſtitutional power, our own hiſtory can ſufficiently inform us. When *Charles* the Second had ſtrengthened himſelf by the return of the garriſon of *Tangier*, " *England* (ſays *Rapin*) ſaw on a ſudden an *amazing revolution*, ſaw herſelf *ſtripped of all her rights and privileges*, excepting ſuch as the king ſhould vouchſafe to grant her: And what is *more aſtoniſhing*, the *Engliſh* themſelves *delivered up* theſe very rights and privileges to *Charles* the Second, which they had ſo *paſſionately*, and, if I may ſay it, *furiouſly* defended againſt the deſigns of *Charles* the Firſt." This hap-pened only *thirty-ſix* years after this laſt prince had been beheaded

SOME

---

† I dont know but it may be ſaid, with a good deal of reaſon, that a quick rotation of miniſters is very deſirable in *Great Britain*. A mi-niſter there has a vaſt ſtore of materials to work with. *Long Adminiſtra-tions* are rather favorable to the *reputation* of a people abroad, than to their *liberty*.

SOME perſons are of opinion, that liberty is not violated, but by ſuch *open* acts of force ; but they ſeem to be greatly miſtaken. I could mention a period within theſe forty years, when almoſt as great a change of diſpoſition was produced by the SECRET meaſures of a *long* adminiſtration, as by *Charles*'s violence. Liberty, perhaps, is never expoſed to ſo much danger, as when the people believe there is the leaſt ; for it may be ſubverted, and yet they not think ſo.

PUBLIC diſguſting acts are ſeldom practiſed by the ambitious, at the beginning of their deſigns. Such conduct *ſilences* and *diſcourages* the weak, and the wicked, who would otherwiſe have been their *advocates* or *accomplices*. It is of great conſequence, to allow thoſe who, upon any account, are inclined to favour them, ſomething ſpecious to *ſay* in their defence. Their power may be fully eſtabliſhed, tho' it would not be ſafe for them to do *whatever they pleaſe*. For there are things, which, at ſome times, even *ſlaves* will not bear. *Julius Cæſar*, and *Oliver Cromwell*, did not dare to aſſume the title of *king*. The *Grand Seignor* dares not lay a *new tax*. The king of *France* dares not be a *proteſtant*. Certain popular points may be left untouched, and yet freedom be extinguiſhed. The commonalty of *Venice* imagine themſelves free, becauſe they are permitted to do what they ought not. But I quit a ſubject, that would lead me too far from my purpoſe.

By the late act of parliament, taxes are to be levied upon us, for " defraying the charge of the *adminiſtration of juſtice*---the ſupport of *civil government*---and the expences of *defending* his Majeſty's dominions in *America*."

IF any man doubts what ought to be the conduct of theſe colonies on this occaſion, I would aſk him theſe queſtions.

HAS

HAS not the parliament *exprefsly* AVOWED their INTENTION of raifing money from us FOR CERTAIN PURPOSES? Is not this fcheme *popular* in *Great-Britain?* Will the taxes, impofed by the late act, *anfwer thofe purpofes?* If it will, muft it not take an *immenfe fum* from us? If it will not, *it is to be expected,* that the parliament will not *fully execute* their INTENTION when it is *pleafing at home,* and *not oppofed here?* Muft not this be done by impofing NEW *taxes?* Will not every addition, thus made to our taxes, be an addition to the power of the *Britifh* legiflature, *by increafing the number of officers* employed in the collection? Will not every additional tax therefore render it *more difficult to* abrogate any of them? When a branch of revenue is once eftablifhed, does it not appear to many people *invidious* and *undutiful,* to attempt to abolifh it? If taxes, fufficient to *accomplifh the* INTENTION of the parliament, are impofed by the parliament, *what taxes will remain* to be impofed by our affemblies? If *no material taxes remain* to be impofed by them, what muft become of *them,* and the *people* they reprefent?

* " IF any perfon confiders thefe things, and yet thinks our liberties are in no danger, I wonder at that perfon's fecurity."

ONE other argument is to be added, which, by itfelf, I hope, will be fufficient to convince the moft incredulous man on this continent, that the late act of parliament is *only* defigned to be a PRECEDENT, whereon the future vaffalage of thefe colonies may be eftablifhed.

EVERY duty thereby laid on articles of *Britifh* manufacture, is laid on fome commodity, upon the exportation of which from *Great-Britain* a *drawback* is
payable

---

* Demofthenes's 2d Philippic.

payable. Those *drawbacks*, in most of the articles, are *exactly double* to the *duties* given by the late act. The parliament therefore might, in *half a dozen lines*, have raised MUCH MORE MONEY, only by *stopping the drawbacks* in the hands of the officers at home, on exportation to these colonies, than by this solemn imposition of taxes upon us, to be collected here. Probably, the artful contrivers of this act formed it in this manner, in order to reserve to themselves, in case of any objections being made to it, this specious pretence---" that the drawbacks are gifts to the colonies, and that the late act only lessons those gifts." But the truth is, that the drawbacks are intended for the encouragement and promotion of *British* manufactures and commerce, and are allowed on exportation to *any foreign parts*, as well as on exportation to these provinces. Besides, care has been taken to slide into the act, some articles on which there are no drawbacks. However, the *whole duties* laid by the late act on *all* the articles therein specified are *so small*, that they will not amount to *as much* as the *drawbacks* which are allowed on *part* of them only. If therefore, *the sum to be obtained by the late act*, had been the *sole object* in forming it, there would not have been any occasion for " the COMMONS of *Great-Britain*, to GIVE and GRANT to his Majesty RATES and DUTIES for *raising a revenue* IN *his Majesty's dominions in* America, for making a more certain and adequate provision for defraying the charges of the administration of justice, the support of civil government, and the expence of defending the said dominions;"---nor would there have been any occasion for an † expensive board of commissioners, and all the other new charges to which we are made liable.

UPON

---

† The expence of this board, I am informed, is between Four and Five Thousand Pound, Sterling a year. The establishment of officers, for collecting the revenue in *America*, amounted before to Seven Thousand six Hundred Pounds *per annum*; and yet, says the author of " The regulation of the colonies," " the whole remittance from all

the

Upon the whole, for my part, I regard the late act as an *experiment made of our disposition*. It is a bird sent out over the waters, to discover, whether the waves, that lately agitated this part of the world with such violence, are yet *subsided*. If *this adventurer* gets footing here, we shall quickly find it to be of the ‡ kind described by the poet----

" *Infelix vates.*"
A direful foreteller of future calamities.

A FARMER.

---

the taxes in the colonies, at an average of *thirty years*, has not amounted to One Thousand Nine Hundred Pounds a year, and in that sum Seven or Eight Hundred Pounds *per annum* only, have been remitted from *North-America*.

The smallness of the revenue arising from the duties in *America*, demonstrates that they were intended only as REGULATIONS OF TRADE : And can any person be so blind to truth, so dull of apprehension in a matter of unspeakable importance to his country, as to imagine, that the board of commissioners lately established at such a charge, is instituted to assist in collecting *One* Thousand Nine Hundred Pounds a year, or the trifling duties imposed by the late act ? Surely every man on this continent must perceive, that they are established for the care of a NEW SYSTEM OF REVENUE, which is but now begun.

‡ " Dira cælæno," &c. *Æneid* 3.

LETTER XII.

My dear COUNTRYMEN,

SOME ftates have loft their liberty by *particular accidents* : But this calamity is generally owing to the *decay of virtue*. A *people* is travelling faft to deftruction, when *individuals* confider *their* interefts as diftinct from *thofe of the public*. Such notions are fatal to their country, and to themfelves. Yet how many are there, fo *weak* and *fordid* as to *think* they perform *all the offices of life*, if they earneftly endeavour to encreafe their own *wealth*, *power*, and *credit*, without the leaft regard for the fociety, under the protection of which they live ; who, if they can make an *immediate profit to themfelves*, by lending their affiftance to thofe, whofe projects plainly tend to the injury of their country, rejoice in their *dexterity*, and believe themfelves entitled to the character of *able politicians*. Miferable men ! Of whom it is hard to fay, whether they ought to be moft the objects of *pity* or *contempt* : But whofe opinions are certainly as *deteftable*, as their practices are *deftructive*.

THO' I always reflect, with a high pleafure, on the integrity and underftanding of my countrymen, which, joined with a pure and humble devotion to the great and gracious author of every blefling they enjoy, will, I hope, enfure to them, and their pofterity, all temporal and eternal happinefs, yet when I confider, that in every age and country there have been bad men, my heart, at this threatening period, is fo full of apprehenfion, as not to permit me to believe, but that there may be fome on this continent, *againft*

whom

whom you ought to be upon your guard---Men, who
either * hold, or expect to hold certain advantages,
by setting examples of servility to their countrymen.
Men, who trained to the employment, or self taught
by

* It is not intended by these words, to throw any reflection upon
gentlemen, because they are possessed of offices. For many of them are
certainly men of virtue, and lovers of their country. But supposed
obligations of *gratitude*, and *honor*, may induce them to be silent.
Whether these obligations *ought to be* regarded or not, is not so much
to be confidered by others, in the judgment they form of these gentlemen, as whether *they think* they ought to be regarded. Perhaps, therefore, we shall act in the properest manner towards them, if we neither
reproach nor *imitate* them. The persons meant in this letter, are the
base spirited wretches, who may endeavour to *distinguish themselves*, by
their sordid zeal in defending and promoting measures, which *they
know, beyond all question*, to be *destructive* to the *just rights* and *true interests* of their country. It is scarcely possible to speak of *these men* with
any degree of *patience*---It is scarcely possible to s'eak of them with any
degree of *propriety*---For no words can truly describe their *guilt* and
meanness---But every honest bosom, on their being mentioned, will
feel what cannot be *expressed*.
   If their wickedness did not blind them, they might perceive along
the coast of these colonies, many men, remarkable instances of wrecked
ambition, who after *distinguishing themselves* in the support of the *Stamp-
Act*, by a courageous contempt of their country, and of justice, have
been left to linger out their miserable existence, without a government,
collectorship, secretaryship, or any o'her commission, to console them
as well as it could, for loss of virtue and reputation---while numberless
offices have been bestowed in these colonies on people from *Great-Britain*, and new ones are continually invented, to be thus bestowed. As
a *few great prizes* are put into a lottery to TEMPT *multitudes to lose*, so
here and there an *American* has been raised to a good post ---
   " *Apparent rari nantes in gurgite vasto.*"
Mr *Greenville*, indeed, in order to recommend the *Stamp Act*, had the
unequalled generosity, to pour down a golden shower of offices upon
Americans; and yet these *ungrateful* colonies did not thank Mr. *Greenville* for shewing his kindness to their countrymen, nor *them* for ac-
cepting it. How must that great statesman have been surprized to
find, that the unpolished colonies could not be reconciled to *infamy* by
treachery? Such a *beautiful* disposition towards us never appeared in
any minister before him, and probably never will appear again. For it
is *evident*, that *such a system* of policy is to be established on this continent, as, in a short time, is to render it utterly unnecessary to use the
least *art* in order to *conciliate* our approbation of any measures. Some
of our countrymen may be employed to *fix chains* upon us, but *they*
will never be permitted to *hold* them afterwards. So that the utmost,
that any of them can expect, is only a *temporary provision*, that *may*
expire in their own time, but which they may *be assured*, will preclude
their children from having any consideration paid to *them*. NATIVES
of *America* must sink into total NEGLECT and CONTEMPT, the moment
that THEIR COUNTRY loses the constitutional powers she now possesses.

by a natural verfatility of genius, ferve as decoys for drawing the innocent and unwary into fnares. It is not to be doubted but that fuch men will diligently beftir themfelves on this and every like octafion, to fpread the infection of their meannefs as far as they can. On the plans *they* have adopted, this is *their* courfe. *This* is the method to recommend themfelves to their *patrons*.

FROM *them* we fhall learn, how *pleafant* and *profitable* a thing it is, to be for our SUBMISSIVE behavior *well fpoken of* at *St. James's*, or *St. Stephen's*; at *Guildhall*, or the *Royal Exchange*. Specious fallacies will be dreft up with all the arts of delufion, to perfuade one colony *to diftinguifh herfelf from another*, by unbecoming condefcenfions, *which will ferve the ambitious purpofes of great men* at home, and therefore will be thought by them *to entitle their affiftants in obtaining them* to confiderable rewards.

OUR fears will be excited. Our hopes will be awakened. It will be inftituated to us, with a plaufible affectation of *wifdom* and *concern*, how *prudent* it is to pleafe the *powerful*------how *dangerous* to provoke them ---and then comes in the perpetual incantation that freezes up every generous purpofe of the foul in cold, inactive expectation- -" that if there is any requeft to be made, compliance will obtain a favorable attention."

OUR *vigilance* and our *union* are *fuccefs* and *fafety*. Our *negligence* and our *divifion* are *diftrefs* and *death*. They are *worfe*----They are *fhame* and *flavery*. Let us equally fhun the benumbing ftillnefs of *overweening floth*, and the feverifh activity of that *ill-informed zeal*, which bufies itfelf in maintaining *little*, *mean*, and *narrow* opinions. Let us, with a truly wife *generofity* and *charity*, banifh and difcourage all *illiberal diftinctions*, which may arife from differences in *fituation*, forms of

N *government,*

government, or modes of *religion*. Let us consider ourselves as MEN---FREEMEN-- CHRISTIAN FREEMEN -- *separated from the rest of the world*, and *firmly bound together* by the *same rights*, *interests* and *dangers*. Let *these* keep our attention inflexibly fixed on the GREAT OBJECTS, which we must CONTINUALLY REGARD, in order to *preserve those rights*, to *promote those interests*, and to *avert those dangers*.

LET these *truths* be indelibly impressed on our minds ---*that we cannot be* HAPPY, *without being* FREE---that we cannot be free, *without being secure in our property*--that *we* cannot be secure in our property, *if, without our consent, others may, as by right, take it away*---that *taxes imposed on us by parliament*, do thus take it away- - that *duties laid for the sole purpose of raising money*, are taxes---that *attempts* to lay such duties *should be instantly and firmly opposed*---that this opposition can never be effectual, *unless it is the united effort of these provinces*--that therefore BENEVOLENCE *of temper towards each other*, and UNANIMITY *of councils*, are essential to the welfare of the whole---and lastly, that for this reason, every man amongst us, who in any manner would encourage either *dissension*, *diffidence*, or *indifference*, between these colonies, is an enemy to *himself*, and to *his country*.

THE belief of these truths, I verily think, my countrymen, is indispensably necessary to your happiness. I beseech you, therefore, § " teach them diligently unto your children, and talk of them when you sit in your houses, and when you walk by the way, and when you lie down, and when you rise up."

WHAT have these colonies to *ask*, while they continue free ? Or what have they to *dread*, but insidious attempts to subvert their freedom ? *Their prosperity* does not depend on *ministerial favours doled* out to par-
ticular

§ Deuteron. vi. 7.

ticular provinces. *They* form *one* political body, of which *each colony* is a *member*. *Their happiness* is founded on *their constitution* ; and is to be promoted, by preserving that constitution in unabated vigor, *throughout every part*. A spot, a speck of decay, however small the limb on which it appears, and however remote it may seem from the vitals, should be alarming. We have *all the rights* requisite for our prosperity. The *legal authority* of *Great-Britain* may indeed lay hard restrictions upon us ; but, like the spear of *Telephus*, it will cure as well as wound. Her unkindness will instruct and compel us, after some time, to discover, in our *industry* and *frugality*, surprising remedies---*if our rights continue unviolated:* For as long as the *products* of our *labor*, and the *rewards* of our *care*, can properly be called *our own*, so long it will be worth our while to be *industrious* and *frugal*. But if when we plow-- sow--- reap---gather---and thresh---we find, that we plow---- sow--- reap---gather--- and thresh *for others*, whose PLEASURE is to be the SOLE LIMITATION *how much* they shall *take*, and *how much* they shall *leave*, WHY should we repeat the unprofitable toil ? *Horses* and *oxen* are content with *that portion of the fruits of their work*, which their *owners* assign them, in order to keep them strong enough to raise successive crops ; but even *these beasts* will not submit to draw for their *masters*, until they are *subdued* by *whips* and *goads*.

LET us take care of our *rights*, and we *therein* take care of *our prosperity*. * " SLAVERY IS EVER PRECEDED BY SLEEP." *Individuals* may be *dependent* on ministers, if they please. STATES SHOULD SCORN IT ;---and if *you* are not wanting *to yourselves*, you will have a *proper regard* paid *you* by *those*, to whom if you are not *respectable*, you will be *contemptible*. But----if *we have already forgot* the *reasons* that urged us, with unexampled unanimity, to exert ourselves

two

* *Montesquieu's* Spirits of Laws, Book 14, Chap 13

two years ago---if *our zeal* for the public good is *worn out* before the *homespun cloaths,* which it caused us to have made---if *our resolutions* are *so faint,* as by our present conduct to *condemn* our own late *successful* example---if *we are not affected* by any reverence for the memory of our ancestors, who transmitted to us that freedom in which they had been blest---if *we are not animated* by any regard for posterity, to whom, by the most sacred obligations, we are bound to deliver down the invaluable inheritance---THEN, indeed, any *minister*---or any *tool* of a minister---or any *creature* of a tool of a minister---or any *lower* ‡ *instrument of* † *administration,* if lower there be, is a *personage* whom it may be dangerous to offend. I

‡ " Inftrumenta regni " *Tacitus's* Ann. *Book* 12, § 66

† If any perfon fhall imagine that he difcovers, in thefe letters, the leaft diflike of the dependence of thefe colonies on *Great-Britain,* I beg that fuch perfon will not form any judgment on *particular expreffions,* but will confider the *tenor of all the letters taken together* In that cafe, I flatter myfelf, that every unprejudiced reader will be *convinced,* that the true interefts of *Great-Britain* are as dear to me, as they ought to be to every good fubject

If I am an *Enthufiaft* in any thing, it is in my zeal for the *perpetual dependence* of thefe colonies on their mother country ----A dependence founded on *mutual benefits,* the continuance of which can be fecured only by *mutual affections* Therefore it is, that with extreme apprehenfion I view the fmalleft feeds of difcontent, which are unwarily fcattered abroad Fifty or Sixty years will make aftonifhing alterations in thefe colonies, and this confideration fhould render it the bufinefs of *Great-Britain* more and more to cultivate our good difpofitions towards her : But the misfortune is, that thofe *great men,* who are wreftling for power at home think themfelves very flightly interefted in the profperity of their country Fifty or Sixty years hence, but are deeply concerned in blowing up a popular clamour for fuppofed *immediate advantages.*

For my part, I regard *Great Britain* as a Bulwark, happily fixed between thefe colonies and the powerful nations of *Europe.* That kingdom remaining fafe, we, under its protection, enjoying peace, may diffufe the bleffings of religion, fcience, and liberty, thro' remote wilderneffes It is therefore inconteftably our *duty,* and our *intereft,* to fupport the ftrength of *Great Britain* When confiding in that ftrength, fhe begins to forget from whence it arofe, it will be an eafy thing to fhew the fource She may readily be reminded of the loud alarm fpread among her merchants and tradefmen, by the univerfal affociation of thefe colonies, at the time of the *Stamp Act,* not to import any of her MANUFACTURES

In the year 1718, the *Ruffians* and *Swedes* entered into an agreement, not to fuffer *Great Britain* to export any NAVAL STORES from their dominions

I SHALL be extremely forry, if any man miſtakes
my meaning in any thing I have ſaid. Officers employed by the crown, are, while according to the laws
they conduct themſelves, entitled to legal obedience,
and ſincere reſpect. Theſe it is a duty to render them;
and theſe no good or prudent perſon will withold. But
when theſe officers, thro' raſhneſs or deſign, deſire to
enlarge their authority beyond its due limits, and expect improper conceſſions to be made to them, from
regard for the employments they bear, their attempts
ſhould be conſidered as equal injuries to the crown and
people, and ſhould be courageouſly and conſtantly oppoſed. To ſuffer our ideas to be confounded by *names*
on ſuch occaſions, would certainly be an *inexcuſable
weakneſs*, and probably an *irremediable error.*

WE have reaſon to believe, that ſeveral of his Majeſty's preſent miniſters are good men, and friends to
our country; and it ſeems not unlikely, that by a particular concurrence of events, we have been treated a
little more ſeverely than they wiſhed we ſhould be.
They might not think it prudent to ſtem a torrent. But
what is the difference to *us*, whether arbitrary acts take
their riſe from miniſters, or are permitted by them?
Ought any point to be allowed to * a good miniſter,
that

minions but in *Ruſſian* or *Swediſh* ſhips, and at their own prices.
Great-Britain was diſtreſſed Pitch and tar roſe to *Three pounds* a barrel.
At length ſhe thought of getting theſe articles from the colonies, and
the attempt ſucceeding, they fell down to *Fifteen ſhillings.* In the year
1756, *Great-Britain* was threatened with an invaſion. An eaſterly
wind blowing for ſix weeks, ſhe could not MAN her fleet, and the whole
nation was thrown into the utmoſt conſternation The wind changed.
The *American* ſhips arrived. The fleets ſailed in ten or fifteen days.
There are ſome other reflections on this ſubject, worthy of the moſt deliberate attention of the *Britiſh* parliament, but they are of ſuch a nature, that I do not chuſe to mention them publicly I thought it my
duty, in the year 1765, while the *Stamp-Act* was in ſuſpence, to write
my ſentiments to a gentleman of great influence at home, who afterwards diſtinguiſhed himſelf, by eſpouſing our cauſe, in the debates
concerning the repeal of that act.
* Ubi imperium ad ignaros aut minus bonos pervenit, *novum illud
exemplum*, ab dignis, & idoneis, ad indignos & non idoneos *transfertur.*
Sall. Bell. Cat. § 50.

that should be denied to a bad one? The mortality of ministers, is a very frail mortality. A ― ―― may suc-ceed a *Shelburne*―A ―――― may succeed a *Conway*.

WE find a new kind of minister lately spoken of at home―" THE MINISTER OF THE HOUSE OF COMMONS." The term seems to have peculiar propriety when refer-red to these colonies, *with a different meaning annexed to it*, from that in which it is taken there. By the word " minister" we may understand not only a *servant of the crown*, but a *man of influence* among the commons, who regard themselves as having a share in the *sove-reignty* over us. The " minister of the house" may, in a point respecting the colonies, be so strong, that the minister of the crown *in* the house, if he is a distinct person, may not choose, even where his sentiments are favorable to us, to come to a pitched battle upon our account. For tho' I have the highest opinion of the deference of the house for the King's minister, yet he may be so good natured, as not to put it to the test, except it be for the mere and immediate profit of his master or himself.

BUT whatever kind of *minister* he is, that attempt to innovate *a single iota* in the privileges of these colonies, him I hope you will *undauntedly oppose*, and that you will never suffer yourselves to be either *cheated* or *fright-ned* into any *unworthy obsequiousness*. On such emer-gencies you may surely, without presumption, believe, that ALMIGHTY GOD himself will look down upon your righteous contest with gracious approbation. You will be a " *band of brothers*," cemented by the dearest ties,―and strengthened with inconceivable sup-plies of force and constancy, by that sympathetic ardor, which animates good men, confederated in a good cause. Your *honor* and *welfare* will be, as they now are, most intimately concerned ; and besides―*you are assigned by divine providence*, in the appointed order of things, the

protectors

protectors of unborn ages, whose fate depends upon your
virtue Whether *they* shall arise the *generous* and *indisputable heirs* of the noblest patrimonies, or the *dastardly* and *hereditary drudges* of imperious task-masters, YOU
MUST DETERMINE.

To discharge this double duty to *yourselves*, and to
your *posterity*, you have nothing to do, but to call forth
into use the *good sense* and *spirit* of which you are possessed. You have nothing to do, but to conduct your
affairs *peaceably---prudently--- firmly-- -jointly*. By *these
means* you will support the character of *freemen*, without
losing that of *faithful subjects*---a good character in any
government----one of the best under a *British* government---You will *prove*, that *Americans* have that true
magnanimity of soul, that can relent injuries, without
falling into rage; and that tho' your devotion to
Great-Britain is the most affectionate, yet you can make
PROPER DISTINCTIONS, and know what you owe *to
yourselves*, as well as *to her*--You will, at the same time
that you advance your *interests*, advance your *reputation*
---You will convince the world of the *justice of your demands*, and the *purity of your intentions*.-----While all
mankind must, with unceasing applauses, confess, that
you indeed DESERVE liberty, who so *well understand* it,
so *passionately love* it, so *temperately enjoy* it, and so
wisely, bravely, and *virtuously assert, maintain*, and *defend* it.

    " *Certe ego libertatem, quæ mihi a parente meo tradita
      est, experiar : Verum id frustra an ob rem faciam, in
      vestra manu situm est, quirites.*"

    FOR my part, I am resolved to contend for the li-
      berty delivered down to me by my ancestors;
      but whether I shall do it effectually or not, de-
      pends on you, my countrymen.

    " How little soever one is able to write, yet when
      the liberties of one's country are threatned, it is
      still more difficult to be silent." .

             A FARMER.

- Is there not the ftrongeft probability, that if the univerfal fenfe of thefe colonies is immediately expreffed by RESOLVES of the affemblies, in fupport of their rights, by INSTRUCTIONS to their agents on the fubject, and by PETITIONS to the crown and parliament for redrefs, thefe meafures will have the fame fuccefs now, that they had in the time of the *Stamp-Aſt.*

D.

F I N I S.

Printed in the USA
CPSIA information can be obtained
at www.ICGtesting.com
LVHW011746211023
761754LV00005B/396